AF600551

ECCLESIASTICAL PROPERTY IN AUSTRALIA AND NEW ZEALAND

The Catholic University of America
Canon Law Studies
No. 387

Ecclesiastical Property in Australia and New Zealand

AN HISTORICAL SYNOPSIS AND COMPARATIVE STUDY OF THE GENERAL LAW OF THE CHURCH, CANONS 1495—1551, AND THE DECREES OF THE FOURTH PLENARY COUNCIL OF AUSTRALIA, DECREES 653—685

A DISSERTATION

SUBMITTED TO THE FACULTY OF THE SCHOOL OF CANON LAW OF THE CATHOLIC UNIVERSITY OF AMERICA IN PARTIAL FULFILLMENT OF THE REQUIREMENTS FOR THE DEGREE OF DOCTOR OF CANON LAW

BY

REV. JAMES E. MUNDAY, J.C.L.

PRIEST OF THE ARCHDIOCESE OF SYDNEY, AUSTRALIA

The Catholic University of America Press
Washington, D.C.
1957

NIHIL OBSTAT:
THOMAS O. MARTIN, Ph.D., S.T.D., J.C.D. LL.B., LLM.
Censor Deputatus
Washingtonii, die 20 maii, 1957

IMPRIMATUR:
✠ NORMAN THOMAS CARDINAL GILROY
Archiepiscopus Sydneyensis

Sydneyensi, die 24 maii, 1957

Printed by The Abbey Press, St. Meinrad, Indiana, U.S.A.

DEDICATED TO
MY FATHER AND MOTHER
AND TO THE
PIONEER BISHOPS, PRIESTS AND RELIGIOUS
IN AUSTRALIA

FOREWORD

The great importance that temporal goods have had in the plan of the Church is seen from the multiplicity and detail of legislation which has marked the efforts of the lawmakers throughout the entire history of the Christian era properly to acquire and faithfully to safeguard the ecclesiastical patrimony. Indeed, there is scarcely any subject more intimately bound up with the history and development of the Church than that of its temporalities. The history of the modes of acquisition and methods of administration of property presents to the student of jurisprudence the story of its vicissitudes and its triumphs. While in many instances the decretal collections and conciliar enactments lack the romantic interest and picturesque grouping that constitute the charm of other topics of its history, a deeper knowledge of the Church's legislation on the acquisition and administration of property throughout the centuries surely gives a better understanding and appreciation of the present law of the Code on these matters.

In Australia the question of ecclesiastical property has lacked, for the most part, the perplexities and problems encountered in Europe and America. Perhaps this is the reason why so little space and so few decrees have been devoted to temporal goods in the first three Plenary Councils. Again, unlike other countries, Australia is so young that, in many ways, the endemic conflicts in evidence between the Church and State elsewhere in the eighteenth and nineteenth centuries have been avoided. Nevertheless, the Church in Australia had its problems, not the least of which was the lack of temporalities and material means efficiently and thoroughly to begin and to pursue its work for the salvation of souls.

The present work, unfortunately, is anything but exhaustive. As the subject matter is almost unlimited the writer has, necessarily, to confine himself to a brief outline of the canons and decrees treated in order to cover, at least in part, every section of ecclesiastical property. Hence, while briefly touching upon the gradual recognition of the individual rights of its members as members of the Church and the development of its juridical status through the English Acts of Emancipation, the dissertation treats of the acquisition and administration of ecclesiastical property in Australia in accordance with the general law of the Church, canons 1495—1551 and the decrees of the Fourth Plenary Council of Australia and New Zealand, held at Sydney, Australia, A.D. 1937, decrees nos. 653—685.

The Code of Canon Law in conjunction with the local statues, customs and provisions as incorporated in the decrees of the Fourth Plenary Council of Australia provide a body of law that is suitably adapted to a country so distant from the Chair of Peter yet so united with it by the bond of faith.

The writer welcomes this occasion to express his gratitude to His Eminence Cardinal Gilroy, Archbishop of Sydney, for leave of absence from the archdiocese for the opportunity of advanced study in Canon Law at the Catholic University of America; to His Excellency, the Most Reverend Patrick A. O'Boyle, Archbishop of Washington, for an appointment as Assistant Priest at St. Joseph's Church during the three years of the university course, and to the Right Reverend Monsignor Edward P. McAdams, Pastor of St. Joseph's, whose kindness and solicitude made the writer's sojourn in Washington so pleasant and rewarding. In particular he is grateful to the Faculty of the School of Canon Law and to all others whose helpful suggestions made this dissertation possible.

TABLE OF CONTENTS

PREFACE

The Church itself decides in its present law[1] the precise meaning of *"church property"* or *"ecclesiastical goods."* They are all temporal goods, corporeal or incorporeal, movable or immovable, which belong to the Church Universal and to the Apostolic See or to some other legal entity in the Church. Though its rights from time to time have been variously infringed it steadfastly maintains, inasmuch as it is a sovereign society, its right to acquire temporal goods. They are a necessary means to the prosecution of the end of its existence. "The Catholic Church and the Apostolic See have the innate right freely and independently of the civil power to acquire, hold and administer temporal goods for the fulfilment of the end for which it was founded."[2]

These temporal goods are actually owned by dioceses, parishes, religious orders and other such legal entities as well as by the Apostolic See and the Universal Church itself, whence ultimately the juridic personality of the former is derived. The Catholic Church as a juridically perfect society possesses personality from the divine law[3] and therefore independently of any positive act of human authority. Its divine right to acquire property is proved solely and sufficiently from its very establishment by Christ as a perfect society.[4] Hence, inasmuch as it does not derive its personality from another source but has it in its own right, it has its own complete sphere of activity independent of local civil law.

The very nature of the Church's work among men de-

[1] *Codex Iuris Canonici*, Pii X Pontificis Maximi iussu digestus, Benedicti XV auctoritate promulgatus (Romae, 1917. Reimpressio, Westminster, Maryland; The Newman Press, 1954), Canon 1497, § 3.

[2] Canon 1495, § 1.

[3] Canon 100, § 1.

[4] Leo XIII, encyl *Immortale Dei*, 1 nov. 1885—*Codicis Iuris Canonici Fontes*, cura Emi Petri Card. Gasparri editi (9 vols., Romae postea Civitate Vaticana: Typis Polyglottis Vaticanis 1923-1939), n. 592 (hereafter cited *Fontes*).

mands that it foster those forms of divine worship that are consistant with the nature of its members. They are not disembodied spirits; they are beings composed of body and soul.[5] Its doctrine must be clothed in forms that satisfy men's hearts and must be vivified with external manifestations of their inner feelings. Thus external and visible means are employed by the Church, as Christ intended, to foster and aid the expression of internal religious sentiments. The offering of the Holy Sacrifice of the Mass, the administration of the sacraments and their consequent religious ceremonies all demand the existence of churches, altars, sacred vessels, vestments and the like. All this indicates the validity of the Church's right to acquire, possess and use whatever is necessary for the attainment of its end.

Likewise, as the Church is a public society with public functions and forms of worship, there is need of ministers to perform these sacred rites. These, too, have need of support, for, as St. Paul says, "the Lord ordained that they who preach the gospel should live by the gospel."[6] "I have taken from other churches, receiving wages of them for your ministry."[7] Moreover, as history abundantly shows, the Church both needed and used its temporal goods to support and protect the poor, "for the poor you always have with you."[8] Since it is subject to the same needs and exigencies as other independent and perfect societies, material goods not only become useful but also lawful and necessary for the continuation of the work of Christ on earth.[9]

The necessity and validity of the Church's possession of temporal goods are indicated by its constant practice since Apostolic times, by its uniform teaching on the subject during the past two millennia, as well as by the consensus

[5] *III Concilium Plenarium Baltimorense* (2. ed., Baltimore: John Murphy, 1894), n. 264.

[6] I Cor., IX:14.

[7] II Cor., XI:8.

[8] Matthew, XXVI:11.

[9] *III Conc. Plen. Baltimor.*, n. 264.

reflected among all Christian peoples. While primarily instructing His disciples and followers in the new way of man's spiritual life, Christ nevertheless did not oppose the right of acquiring property, nor did He fail to guide them in the use and administration of whatever temporal goods came to them. Thus He appointed Judas in charge of the purse, from which their daily needs were supplied.[10] St. Peter, too, He commissioned to pay the tribute.[11]

Commenting on this, St. Augustine clearly expounded the teaching of Christ and the Church: "The Lord, therefore, had also a money box, where He kept the offerings of believers. These offerings He employed in relief of His own needs and of the needs also of others. It was then that the custom of having Church money was first introduced, so that thereby we might understand that His precept about taking no thought for the morrow was not a command that no money should be kept by His saints, but that God should not be served for any such end, and that the doing of what is right should not be held in abeyance through fear of want."[12]

The early Apostolic Church in acquiring the necessary temporal goods merely followed the example of its Divine Founder. It needed resources to carry on its work and appealed to its fervent members to give of their surplus goods for the alleviation of poverty, and to be generous in their support of God's ministers, who for their ministering in the holy places had the right "to eat the things that are of the holy place and partake with the altar."[13]

These principles and premises, however, along with the historical basis of the Church's rights, were not always recognized. As the Church evolved and grew century by century, so did its material possessions. So, too, did the

[10] John, XII:6; XIII:29.

[11] Matthew, XVII:26.

[12] *In Evang. Joann.*, Tract. LXII, n. 5—Migne, *Patrologiae Cursus Completus, Series Latina* (221 vols., Paris 1844-55), XXXV, 1805 (hereafter cited *MPL*).

[13] I Cor., IX:13.

avarice and envy of the civil powers, ever ready speedily to enrich themselves through the expropriation of ecclesiastical goods. History shows in every age its rights infringed and its property confiscated.

In England after the reformation, not only its legal status but even its very right to existence was denied.[14] Not only was church property expropriated by the crown, but the faithful, like sheep scattered by ravenous wolves, were dispersed, even to far-off lands. In the colonies, especially Australia, founded centuries later, a more radical problem was encountered. There were no material reminders of former glory or of legal status as in England. Catholics were few. They had no history, no tradition other than the faith of their fathers. Indeed, for the first forty years of Australian history, the juridical existence of the Catholic Church, its very right to exist, even more than its right to possess and administer property or goods of any kind, was in question.

[14] Hilaire Belloc, *How The Reformation Happened* (New York; Dodd, Mead & Co., Inc. 1954).

PART I
HISTORICAL SYNOPSIS

CHAPTER I

HISTORICAL INTRODUCTION

ARTICLE 1. THE FOUNDING OF AUSTRALIA

The growth and development of the Church in Australia is amazing and gratifying. Its humble beginning is reminiscent of the Church in Roman times. Like the grain of mustard seed soon to grow into a tree in which the birds of the air may dwell, so has it flourished in this "Terra Australis" or "Land of the South Star." Its adherents are now fast approaching the two million mark, while its churches, schools and manifold material appurtenances are numbered by many thousands.[1] Such extraordinary growth has been due under the Holy Spirit to numerous factors. Not only did persecution, privation and hardship strengthen the faith brought by the first settlers and Irish political prisoners, but, later still, valiant and steadfast leaders, bishops, priests and devoted missionary sisters nurtured, tended and transplanted the seed of faith, ever ready to flourish in such fertile soil.

The spiritual and material success of modern times, however, along with the prestige and the ever-growing status that the Church now enjoys, would hardly have been envisioned even by the most optimistic of the first inhabitants. Such was the isolation and so great the distance either way from the civilization of those times that truly it was the end of the earth to which they were transported. Indeed, the inertia, the hopelessness almost of their position, engendered both by nostalgia and the prison-like atmosphere and the treatment of military guards, was hardly conducive to the speedy establishment of a self-supporting community. Such were the humble circumstances of the first Catholic arrivals in Australia.

[1] *Australasian Catholic Directory, 1956* (Sydney, Pellegrini & Co. Pty. Ltd., 1956), p. 498.

The "Columbus of the South Seas" was the illustrious De Quiros, who, on December 8, 1605, set out from Callao on his last voyage of discovery. With orders from the Spanish court and with letters from the reigning pontiff Pope St. Pius V, conveying the latter's blessing, the expedition sought to extend the boundaries of Christ's spiritual kingdom. On the feast of Pentecost, 1606, De Quiros saluted from afar what appeared to him to be the great southern continent for which he was searching, and he gave to it, in honour of the feast which was that day celebrated, the name "Tierra Austral del Espiritu Santo," which has been justly translated "Australia of the Holy Ghost."[2]

The significance and the value of this discovery was, however, neglected by the Spaniards, and it was not until 1770, over 150 years later, that Captain James Cook in his ship, the "Endeavour," sailed along the thousands of miles of the fertile shores of the continent and later persuaded the reluctant British Government of the advantages that would accrue to the empire from the possession and colonization of the eastern coasts of Australia. But again, notwithstanding the interest awakened by these discoveries, it seemed as if, amid the maelstrom of war and domestic strife, the southern continent was destined soon to be forgotten.

England and France were the only great powers that could engage in colonization in those days. The energies of France, however, were absorbed in the throes of her social and political revolution, while England herself was engaged in what appeared to be a death struggle with her American colonies. Hence, strange as it may seem, the Declaration of American Independence broke the spell which for so long had bound this southern continent. The convicts, political, religious and otherwise, could no longer be sent across the Atlantic. Another penal settlement had of necessity to be chosen. Botany Bay was the place selected

[2] Patrick Francis Cardinal Moran, *History of The Catholic Church in Australasia* (2 vols., Sydney, Australia: The Oceanic Publishing Co. Ltd., 1895), I, 2.

by Great Britain. In 1788 Governor Phillip, commanding a fleet of ten ships with 1,030 souls, including 697 convicts, came to claim the land in the name of the reigning sovereign, King George III.[3]

Article 2. The Church in Australia in the 19th Century

There are four distinct periods in the history of the Church during the first century of Australia's existence. The first embraces a little more than thirty years, from the beginning of the convict settlement until the arrival of Fathers Therry and Connolly in 1820; and second from that date to the middle of the century; the third until 1880; and the fourth until Federation in 1901.[4]

During the first period the Church had no official or legal status at all. As the new colony was an English settlement all English law was applicable. Catholic Emancipation was not yet a reality. As there were no priests, there were neither churches nor schools. A few convict priests administered the consolations of religion, for the most part stealthily, to the suffering members of the scattered flock. The one free priest, Father Jerimiah O'Flynn, who ventured to devote his life to them, was imprisoned and afterwards banished.

The English Government neglected even the official religion. Only after repeated remonstrances and at the last minute was a Methodist minister, Rev. Mr. Johnston, named as chaplain to the settlement. He proved unequal to his task and of such little energy that after four years in the colony he still had no church. Writing to the Governor in 1792, he stated: "We have been here now above four years and the first time we had public service at Port Jackson I found things much more comfortable for myself and the congregation than I did last Sunday."[5]

All land belonged to the crown. It could be obtained only through a grant from the Governor by those acceptable to

[3] Moran, *op. cit.*, I, 3. [4] Moran, *ibid.*, p. 23. [5] *Ibid.*, p. 8.

him. As the Church of England was the only official church, it was the only one able to obtain land on which a church could be built. Trade was carried on by barter, and workmen who were not convicts were paid in kind. Convicts were not paid at all. The first church of any kind erected in Australia, made of posts, wattle, cabbage trees and mud plaster and thatched with cabbage tree leaves, was paid for in rum, flour, pork, beef, tobacco and tea. Governor Hunter in 1802 ordered two churches built at Parramatta and Sydney. These, along with 400 acres of land given as a glebe, seem to be the first official church property of any description in Australia. Not only were Catholic convicts forced to attend these two churches, but also their children, classified as "orphans," were made to attend the orphan school and were brought up as Protestants.[6]

In the early part of the nineteenth century, the local government of New South Wales promulgated a regulation that the whole prison population, indiscriminately, should attend the Church of England, under penalty of twenty-five lashes for the first refusal, fifty for the second, and transportation to another penal settlement for the third refusal.[7]

In his account of the colony of New South Wales, Lt. Colonel Collins wrote: "The discharge of religious duties was never omitted, Divine Service being performed every Sunday that the weather would permit, at which time the detachment of marines paraded with their arms, and the whole body of convicts attended."[8]

The severity of these regulations, however, was gradually relaxed, so that by 1820 some little freedom was granted to Catholics and non-conformists.[9]

The second period in the history of the Church in Aus-

[6] *Loc. cit.*

[7] Mr. Justice R. Therry, *Reminiscences of New South Wales* (London, 1863), p. 145.

[8] Lt. Col. D. Collins, "Account of the Colony of New South Wales from January 1788 to August 1801," as quoted in Moran, *History of the Catholic Church in Australia,* I, 19.

[9] Moran, *History of the Catholic Church in Australia,* I, 25.

tralia was one of partial tolerance, and it witnessed a measure of official freedom extended to the Catholic Church. This was the result of the Acts of Emancipation in England in 1829.[10] It was an epoch-making period insofar as Australia's first bishop, John Bede Polding, O.S.B., was consecrated in England on June 29, 1834, and was made Archbishop on April 10, 1842.[11]

So quickly did the number of faithful and clergy increase after 1830 that in 1844 the First Provincial Council of Australia was held at Sydney. It was presided over by Archbishop Polding and attended by his two suffragan bishops, Robert William Willson, Bishop of Hobart, and Francis Murhpy, Bishop of Adelaide, and thirty-three priests of the newly established dioceses.

Edictum. De Concilio Provinciali in Australia Primo.

Joannes Beda Archiepiscopus.

> Cum pro nostro Archiepiscopali officio et munere, et antiquorum et in sacro Tridentino consilio editorum canonum observatione ad moderandos, mores, corrigendos excessus, controversias componendas, aliaque a Sacris Canonibus permissa Provinciale Consilium convocare debeamus, Reverendissimos Provinciae nostrae Episcopos die IV. Idus Septembris per literas nominatim ad singulos scriptas ad synodum in nostra Sydniensi Metropolitana Ecclesia sub Titulo S. Mariae Virginis evocavimus. Ut autem aliis etiam omnibus qui de iure debent interesse nota sit huius concilii celebratio, idcirco universis et singulis per hoc Edictum quod Ecclesiae Metropolitanae valvis affigi jussimus Provincialis Concilii futuram celebrationem significavimus. In quorum fidem hoc Edictum confici et per Secretarium nostrum inscribi et nostri sigilli impressione muniri volumus. Datum Sydneii, die 3 Septembris, 1844. De

[10] *Act for the Better Securing of the Charitable Donations and Bequests of His Majesty's Subjects in Great Britain Professing the Roman Catholic Religion*—2 & 3 Wm. IV, c. 115 (1832).

[11] *Acta et Decreta Concilii Primi Provinciae Australiensis, A.D. MDCCCXLIV* (Sydney; F. Cunninghame & Co., 1847), p. 6.

mandato Illustrissimi et Reverendissimi Archiepiscopi.

H. G. Gregory, Benedict: in Australia Superior, Secretarius[12]

This third period, that of nominal religious equality, commenced about the year 1865, and continued for a little over thirty years.[13] It was, however, only a nominal religious equality. Despite repeated declarations that all religions are equal before the law, many of the men who wielded political influence over the state displayed an intense bitterness against everything Catholic. Nevertheless, churches and church membership, naturally and through immigration, increased by leaps and bounds during the next quarter of the century, so much so that by 1868 another Provincial Council was considered necessary by the Australian Bishops, now numbering nine. The Council was scheduled to be held at St. Mary's Cathedral, Sydney. Owing to the disasterous fire, however, and the complete destruction of the recently completed Mother Church on January 5, 1869, the generosity and hospitality of the Bishop and Catholic people of Melbourne were extended to the prelates and fathers of the council. Thus the Second Provincial Council of Australia was held at Melbourne, April 17-25, 1869.

The Council's agenda were listed under five headings:

1. What must be done about the newly introduced and government sponsored secular educational system, and how are the evils emerging from it to be combatted.
2. What practices are to be introduced and what conditions to be observed in permitting mixed marriages.
3. How are bishops and the clergy to be remunerated and ecclesiastical goods to be administered.
4. Whether, in order to further vocations for the various dioceses of the Australian Province, it is expedient to establish a common seminary called a "Provincial Seminary."

[12] *Acta et Decreta Concilii Primi Provinciae Australiensis, A.D. MDCCCXLIV*, p. 5.

[13] Moran, *History of the Catholic Church in Australia*, I, 25.

5. What means are to be used to promote and further, as far as possible, the eternal salvation and standard of living of the Australian aborigines.[14]

The fourth period of the history of the Australian Church witnessed its emergence as the second largest (numerically about 25%) religious denomination in the country. The Church asserted its right to a footing of equality with the others, and was strong enough to insist that such a just claim was respected. This was the period, also, of the first two Plenary Councils of the Church in Australia in 1885 and 1895.

DECRETUM S.C. DE PROPAGANDA FIDE.

Ex quo Consilium Secundum Provinciale Anno 1869 in Australia habitum fuit, Ecclesia Catholica iis in regionibus majora coepit incrementa ac fidelium numerus mirum in modum excrevit. Porro ad illud rei Catholicae incrementum magis magisque provehendum Sanctissimum Dominus Noster Leo, divina providentia Papa XIII, illarum regionum Praesules ad novam plenariam synodum habendam invitavit, in qua, spectata praesenti Christianitatis illius conditione, ad res ecclesiasticas ordinatius evolvendas ab iisdem opportuna ederentur decreta. Hinc mense Novembris 1885 Archiepiscopi et Episcopi Australiae Sydney convenerunt ac Praeside ex Apostolica delegatione Eminentissimo ac Reverendissimo Patricio Francisco Moran Cardinali Archiepiscopo Sydneyensi, Sacra Synodus solemniter habita fuit et non pauca, tum ad ecclesiasticam doctrinam firmandam, tum ad abusus evellendos, tum ad Catholicae juventutis institutionem fovendam, tum ad Episcoporum electionem ac rerum temporalium administrationem magis magisque ordinandam, tum denique ad fidem conservandam et dilatandam valde utilia constituta, eaque omnia ad hanc Sacram Congregationem, ut ejus examini subjicerentur, transmissa sunt. Itaque Eminentissimi Patres Sacro Consilio Christiano Nomini Propagando praepositi in

[14] *Acta et Decreta Concilii Secundi Provinciae Australiensis, A.D. 1869* (Sydney, F. Cunninghame & Co., 1870), p. 30.

generalibus comitiis habitis diebus 21 et 22 Martii necnon 4 Aprilis anni 1887 diligenti inquisitione adhibita Decreta ejusdem Concilii expenderunt et nonnullis emendationibus ac modificationibus adjectis, eadem recognoverunt.

Hanc autem Sacrae Congregationis sententiam Summo Pontifici Leoni XIII. a Reverendo Patre Domino Dominico Jacobini ejusdem Sacrae Congregationis Secretario in Audientia diei 24 Aprilis 1887 relatam Sanctitas Sua approbare dignata est, et super his praesens Decretum expediri mandavit.

Datum Romae ex Aedibus Sacrae Congregationis de Propaganda Fide, die 1 Maji 1887.

JOANNES CARDINALIS SIMEONI,
Praefectus.

Dominicus, Archiepiscopus Tyrensis,
Secretarius.[15]

The end of the nineteenth century saw the Church fully organized, with one Cardinal Archbishop, five archiepiscopal sees, and sixteen suffragan bishoprics.[16] Its educational system was wholly religious and completely autonomous. While it could and, indeed, often did happen that the Catholic citizen was practically excluded from certain privileges to which he was entitled, nevertheless, by the time of Federation in 1901, the Church was socially and legally established in the Australian Commonwealth. Near the turn of the century the Church in Australia pursued untrammeled its mission of blessing and mercy[17]

ARTICLE 3. THE RECEPTION AND THE APPLICATION OF THE COMMON LAW OF ENGLAND IN AUSTRALIA

Whenever new colonies were occupied and settled, the English view was that the British colonists took with them

[15] *Acta et Decreta Concilii Plenarii Australasiae, Habiti apud Sydney A.D. 1885, a Sancta Sede Recognita* (Sydney, F. Cunninghame & Co., 1887), p. iii.

[16] *Ibid.*, p. XIII.

[17] Moran, *History of the Catholic Church in Australia*, I, 25.

the common law and statutes of England as far as these were applicable to conditions in the new colony.[18]

It early became the legal theory that the Australian colonies were founded by settlement or occupation. Two points, however, had been argued against this: First, it was stated that Australia was conquered from the Aborigines. This, however, was never taken seriously, as there was no settled body of aboriginal law that could be applied to the economic transactions and social conditions of a more advanced community. Secondly, it was argued that New South Wales, founded in 1789, was not intended to be an ordinary colony, but rather was envisaged as a penal settlement. It seems obvious, therefore, that the laws of England had to be applied out of necessity. This matter was finally settled, in 1828, when the English Parliament provided that "all laws and statutes in force within the realm of England on July 25, 1828, should be applied in the administration of justice in the courts of New South Wales and Van Diemen's land respectively so far as the same could be applied within the said colonies."[19]

With regard to the development of Australian law, Dr. Woinarski points out two theories: one puts the emphasis on English law and endeavours to distinguish what is general and what is merely of local significance; the other puts the emphasis on the circumstances in New South Wales in 1828 and by that test determines whether the particular law is applicable. These theories, however, are "equivalent in substance," no matter how their forms may differ. "Laws in their nature general are suitable to an infant colony: laws suitable to an infant colony are not the artificial requirements peculiar to England."[20]

According to this latter theory it seems that the Act for

[18] G. W. Paton, *The Commonwealth of Australia, The development of its Laws and Constitutions* (London: Stevens & Sons Ltd. 1952) (hereafter cited *The Commonwealth of Australia*).

[19] 9 George IV, c. 82, sec. 24 (1829).

[20] Dr. S. H. Z. Woinarski, *An Introduction to the History of Legal Institutions in Victoria.* (Doctoral Thesis yet to be published),

the Relief of His Majesty's Roman Catholic Subjects[21] was received in New South Wales. Though this act had little or nothing directly to do with ecclesiastical property in England, and hence in New South Wales, nevertheless it was an extensive relaxation of the former law in regard to the civil activity of Catholic subjects. It gave them a status that led later to the abrogation of statutes preventing the Church as a corporate body from owning, using and alienating property for purposes of Religious Worship, Education and Charity. Roman Catholics, upon taking the oath, could now sit and vote in Parliament. They could vote at elections, and hold civil and military offices under His Majesty.[22] They could also be members of Lay Corporations.[23]

Thus, with Catholic Emancipation secured in Great Britain, the colony of New South Wales could also legally grant it. With the Act of August 15, 1832, *"for the Better Securing of the Charitable Donations and Bequests of His Majesty's Subjects in Great Britain Professing the Roman Catholic Religion,"* Roman Catholics became subject to the same laws as Protestant Dissenters with respect to schools and places of worship.

> Be it therefore enacted by the King's most Excellent Majesty, by and with the Advice and Consent of the Lords Spiritual and Temporal, and Commons, in this present Parliament assembled, and by the authority of the same, that from and after passing of this Act His Majesty's Subjects professing the Roman Catholic Religion, in respect to their Schools, Places for Religious Worship, Education and Charitable Purposes, in Great Britain, and the Property held therewith, and the persons employed in or about the same, shall in respect thereof be subject to the same laws as the Protestant Dissenters are subject to in England in respect to their Schools and Places for Religious

[21] 19 George IV, c. 7. (1829).

[22] *Act for the Relief of His Majesty's Roman Catholic Subjects.* 10 George IV, c. 7. sec. 10 (1829).

[23] *Act for the Relief of His Majesty's Roman Catholic Subjects.* 10 George IV, c. 7. sec. 14 (1829).

Worship, Education and Charitable Purposes, and not further or otherwise.[24]

Property held, however, for the purposes mentioned in this Act in England and Wales was to be subject to the provisions of 9 George II, c. 36, provided always "that all Property to be acquired or held for such purposes of Religious Worship, Education, and Charitable Purposes, in England and Wales, shall be subject to the Provisions of an Act passed in the Ninth Year of the Reign of King George the Second, intituled 'An Act to restrain the Disposition of Lands' whereby the same may become unalienable, and to the same Laws as the Protestant Dissenters are subject to in England in respect of the acquiring or holding of such property."[25]

Henceforth any religious body or "Church" recognized by law was protected in the enjoyment of its endowments, and it was the duty of a court of justice to give effect to the intent of the founder of any charity for the benefit of such a body in so far as that could be done apart from all infringement on any known rule of law. The word "Church" was used of any ecclesiastical organism or religious body which was complete within itself. "Church" had two distinct meanings. It could mean either the aggregate of the individual members of the Church, or it could mean the quasi-corporate institution which carries on the religious work of the denomination whose name it bears.[26]

The extent to which such organisms were recognized by the state could be gauged by reference to the statutory facilities afforded to any congregation or society or body of persons associated for any religious purpose.[27]

Statutory facilities were also provided for the convey-

[24] 2 & 3 Wm. IV, c. 115 (1832).

[25] *Act for the Better Securing of the Charitable Donations and Bequests of His Majesty's Subjects in Great Britain Professing the Roman Catholic Religion.* 2 & 3 Wm. IV, c. 115 (1832).

[26] *Halsbury's Laws of England*, Vol. XI Hailsham's 2. ed., (London: Butterworth & Co., 1933) Hailsham, (hereafter cited, *Halsbury's Laws of England*).

[27] *Trustee Appointment Act*, 13 & 14 Vict. c. 28, sec. 1 (1850).

ing or assuring of property acquired by, or by trustees in connection with, any congregation or society or body of persons associated for religious purposes, so that the conveyance or assurance could vest the estate not only in the parties named therein as trustees, but also in their successors in office for the time being.[28]

While in England all religious bodies enjoyed the same general recognition by law, in the State in New South Wales the Catholic Church had no legal entity before 1828 other than at the pleasure of the Governor. The long series of Statutes passed in the centuries succeeding the disruption of the ties between England and the See of Rome had, in spite of numerous appeals, left many traces of the conflict. Thus, while legally the individual Catholic was of equal status with any other citizen, bigotry oftentimes precluded his admission to a responsible office. Nevertheless, theoretically at least, Roman Catholics, whether lay or clerical, were not barred from acting as teachers or schoolmasters.[29] The Catholic clergy, furthermore, were protected from molestation while conducting a religious service in any place of public worship wherein they were authorized to preach, or in any burial ground.[30]

The recognition of the Roman Catholics as a body, however did not involve any recognition of the hierarchy under which they were organized, except upon the basis of consent. While, however, the hierarchy was not re-established in England until 1850, the Home Government in 1834 saw fit to allow for Australia the appointment of the first bishop of the new colony with an official salary of 150 pounds *per annum*.[31] Despite a tremendous storm of protest, this salary was later raised to 500 pounds *per annum*.[32]

The Catholic schools were all primary schools, and their

[28] 13 & 14 Vict. c. 28, sec. 1 (1850), as amended by *Trustee Appointment Act*, 32 & 33 Vict. c. 26 (1869).

[29] *Roman Catholic Relief Act*, 10 George IV, c. 7, sec. 16 (1829).

[30] *Places of Religious Worship Act*, 52 George II, c. 32, sec. 5.

[31] Moran, *History of the Catholic Church in Australia*, I, 183.

[32] *Ibid.*, p. 194.

whole support came from the government. The government also contributed to the salary paid to the teachers, generally a little more than one pound for each child *per annum.*[33]

The relaxation and amendment of the English statute law was anticipated by the enactments in the colony of New South Wales. Almost twenty years before the *Liberty of Religious Worship Act of 1855,*[34]extending the *Roman Catholic Charities Act of 1832*[35] the ex-governor of the colony, Sir Richard Bourke, defended the official attitude and financial support of the Catholic Church generally. He was instrumental, furthermore, in securing the passage of the Church Act in 1836 for the colony, facilitating the erection of places of worship and the appointment of ministers of religion.[36]

The Roman Catholic Charities Act of 1832 allowed property held by Roman Catholics in connection with their places of worship or their schools, or for other educational purposes, to be considered on the same footing as that of the Protestant Dissenters. All property, however, to be acquired or held for any such purposes was subject to the provisions of the *Mortmain and Charitable Uses Act of 1888.*[37]

Trusts for Roman Catholic Charities were ascertained, in the absence of written documents, by their specific usage during the latest period of twenty years in which such usage had been consistent.[38]

Bequests and gifts for the establishment of Roman Catholic bishops, for maintenance and support of colleges, chapels and schools, the Roman Catholic Church, and for the general promotion of the Roman Catholic religion, were

33 *Ibid.*, p. 191.
34 18 & 19 Vict. c. 86, sec. 2.
35 2 & 3 Wm. IV, c. 115, sec. 1.
36 Moran, *History of the Catholic Church in Australia*, I, 197.
37 *Roman Catholic Charities Act*, 51 & 52 Vict. c. 42.
38 *Roman Catholic Charities Act*, 23 & 24 Vict. c. 134, sec. 5

held to be valid as early as 1834.[39] Similarly, it was held in 1860 that any trusts or bequests for the exclusive benefit of the Roman Catholic Church were not to be ruled invalid by reason only of the inclusion in the trust of a gift of a superstitious or prohibited character.[40] The arbiter in such cases was to be the High Court of Justice, or the Charity Commissioners, or the Board of Education, if in the latter case endowments were made solely for educational purposes.[41]

All the above noted Acts theoretically were applicable to Australia. In practice some were anticipated, others ignored. As has already been stated, New South Wales was settled in 1789. Tasmania was separated from the latter in 1825, Victoria in 1851, and Queensland in 1859; but in all cases 1828 remains the date for the reception of English Law. Western Australia was first settled in 1839, and South Australia was founded in 1834. In these states the date of reception was the date of the foundation. The degree of legislative power was gradually extended: first it was representative government, and then it was full responsible government that was introduced.[42]

The states were independent sovereignties subject only (a) to the overriding powers of the Imperial Parliament, and (b) to a doctrine that there was no power to pass laws which were repugnant or inimical to the laws of England. Religion and church property were not mentioned in any local legislative council acts, and were more or less left to the good will of the respective governors. The rather vague principle of being subject to the overriding powers of the Home Government or Imperial Parliament, and of laws being compatible to those of England, could be so interpreted as to prevent any change at all. This led to the *Colonial Laws Validity Act of 1865*, which abolished the

[39] *Bradshaw v. Tasken*, 2 My. & K. 221 (1834); *West v. Shuttleworth*, 2 My & K. 684 (1835).

[40] *Roman Catholic Charities Act*, 23 & 24 Vict. c. 134, sec. 1 (1860).

[41] Hailsham, *Halsbury's Laws of England*, XI, 995.

[42] G. W. Paton, *The Commonwealth of Australia*, p. 6.

theory that colonial legislation must respect the basic principles of English Law, although it declared that a colonial law should be invalid to the extent that it was repugnant to a statute of the Imperial Parliament extending to the colony.[43]

The Commonwealth, or Federation, was established in 1901, and brought with it delicate questions as to the divisions of powers. Nevertheless, the Australian Founders deliberately rejected the American and Continental device of embodying the protection of individual rights and liberties in rigid constitutional guarantees. None such appear in the state constitutions, with the exception of a guarantee of religious toleration in the Tasmanian Constitution Act. Likewise, the Federal Constitution guarantees freedom to all religions.[44]

This is interpreted, as in the United States of America, as protecting only those religious doctrines which do not conflict with the prevailing moral views and the military security of the nation.[45]

Australia, unlike England, has no established church. All are equal before the law in the sense of the above listed interpretation.

[43] *Loc. cit.*

[44] *Australian Constitution,* sec. 116 (1901).

[45] G. W. Paton, *The Commonwealth of Australia,* p. 70 (*Case of Jehovah's Witnesses,* 67 C.L.R. 116), (1943).

PART II

CANONICAL AND DECRETAL COMMENTARY

CHAPTER II

THE TENURE OF ECCLESIASTICAL PROPERTY

Article 1. The Church's Right to Acquire Property

The tenet of the Church's present law, that freely and independently of any civil power it has the right to acquire temporal goods, is generally recognized in every civilized country today. The principles of equity and justice that form the basis of civilized law naturally safeguard the Church's rights also. No one can reasonably question the right of individuals to acquire and own property. Likewise the individual may use his right to group with others and form a society or a corporation, provided this latter is not subversive to the common good.[1]

As the individual, so also groups of individuals, or legally organized corporations, have the right to acquire property.[2] If a corporation is to exist at all and further its ends, it necessarily has the obligation of supporting itself, obtaining its funds lawfully and paying its way generally. This is the *modus operandi* of collegiate groups or corporations or moral personalities today. So, too, has it been the Church's procedure down through the centuries. In canon 1495, § 1, this, its right, is stated absolutely. "The Catholic Church and the Apostolic See have the innate right, freely and independently of the civil power, to acquire, hold and administer temporal goods to further the end proper to itself."

The Church's right is enunciated in language that has been used in decrees and in condemnations in the seemingly endless conflict with heretics and usurpers of ecclesiastical goods. The Church vindicated its rights against and con-

[1] F. Cavagnis, *Institutiones Iuris Publici Ecclesiastici* (4. ed., 3 vols., Romae, 1906), III, n. 377.

[2] Leo XIII, ep. encycl. *Immortale Dei*, 1 nov., 1885—*Fontes*, n. 492; Leo XIII, litt. encycl. *Rerum novarum*, 15 maii, 1891—*Fontes*, n. 611.

demned the errors of Arnold of Brescia (1139), of the Waldenses (1210), of Marsilius of Padua (1327) and of Wycliffe in England, who taught that Christ Himself forbade the acquisition of temporal goods.[3] Similarly did it declare its position against the Gallicans and the Regalists, who held that the Church had no inherent right to temporal goods, but received it by way of concession from the civil power.[4] Pope Martin V in the Council of Constance (1418) condemned several propositions of Wycliffe and of others who impugned the Church's right to temporal goods,[5] while the Gallicans and the Regalists were similarly proscribed by Pius IX in his *Syllabus* of condemned propositions in 1864.[6]

In canon 1495, § 1, the term "Catholic Church" points to the visible and perfect society founded by Christ for rendering the divine worship that is due to God and for sanctifying and saving men.[7] This society is constituted as a juridical personality. The "Apostolic See" is understood in line with the explanation offered in canon 7, and it contemplates not only the Roman Pontiff but also the Roman Curia, which consists of congregations, tribunals and offices through which the Pope carries on the business of the Universal Church.[8]

The Church has an "innate right," a right that is congenital to the Church, that arises from the Church's very

[3] Franciscus Xaverius Wernz-Petrus Vidal, *Ius Canonicum,* Vol. IV, *De Rebus* Pars II Romae: Apud Aedes Universitatis Gregorianae, 1935), p. 191.

[4] Pius IX, Syllabus Errorum (a. 1864), Prop. 26, 27—*Fontes,* n. 543; L. Rivet, *Institutiones Iuris Ecclesiastici* (2 vols., Romae, 1914), II, 14.

[5] Prop. 10, 32, 36—*Fontes,* n. 43.

[6] Pius IX, ep. encycl *Quanta cura,* 8 dec. 1864, prop. 26, 27—Denzinger-Bannwart-Umberg, *Enchiridion Symbolorum Definitionum, et Declarationum de Rebus Fidei et Morum* (editio vigesima sexta emendata et aucta, Friburgi Brisgoviae: Herder and Co., 1947), nn. 1726, 1727.

[7] Udalricus Beste, *Introductio in Codicem* (3. ed., Collegeville, Minn.: St. John's Abbey Press, 1946), p. 738.

[8] Beste, *op. cit.,* p. 738.

nature, that is introduced by divine institution, and that is not acquired or derived in any way from an outside source. The Church enjoys the free and independent right of exercising its legitimate prerogatives so long as they are just and equitable. The object of the Church's right to temporal goods consists materially in its capacity to acquire, hold and administer such temporal goods, both movable and immovable, and formally in the actual acquiring, holding and administering of them in the prosecution of the end proper to itself.[9]

This innate right, then, bars all infringement upon it by the civil power. The right of the latter cannot be absolute, for God alone is the Supreme Lord of the universe; neither can it be unlimited, for the state has the right to temporal goods only in so far as they are necessary for the pursuit of its own ends to the exclusion of all disregard for the rights of others. As the ends of the Church and of the state differ from each other, there should be no conflict, each society adhering to its own proper sphere. In point of fact, however, many such conflicts have arisen. Transgressions on the part of civil powers have been not infrequent. The iniquitous statutes of mortmain menaced and manacled the Church in England for many centuries. This drastic legislation was enacted with a view to depriving the Church of its capacity to inherit and alienate property. As early as 1279 and 1289 these discriminatory laws appeared.[10]

The restraining measures contained in the mortmain statutes originated in feudal times. Kings and feudal lords were envious of the Church's property holdings which were being consistently increased and added to by the liberality of the faithful. They considered the ecclesiastical tenure of property to be inconsistent with the feudal tenure, and thus there arose the mortmain statutes. They were so called because it was said that land conveyed to ecclesiastical corporations was held in a dead hand, which did not lift itself

[9] Beste, *loc. cit.*

[10] F. Pollock-F. W. Maitland, *History of English Law before the Time of Edward I* (2 vols., Cambridge, 1895), I, 315.

to pass the property on to others. The effect of these statutes was to prevent such conveyances.[11]

Mortmain statutes were never applicable in Australia. Indeed, they could never be applied because of the absence of great religious corporations, and also because of the fact that the feudal system had long been outdated at the time of the founding of Australia. The statutes that did remain in England were counteracted as early as 1834 when "bequests and gifts for the establishment of Roman Catholic bishops, for the maintenance and support of colleges, chapels and schools, for the Roman Catholic Church, and for the general practice of the Roman Catholic religion," were held to be valid.[12]

The right of the Church in general to hold and administer property is extended also to individual churches. Canon 1495, §2, states: "Moreover, in accordance with the norms of the sacred canons the right of acquiring, owning and administering property belongs also to individual churches and to other moral persons which have been established as juridical persons by ecclesiastical authority." This has been the universal practice since the earliest days of the Church. Individual parishes, churches and other ecclesiastical corporations were cognizant of their capacity and right to acquire goods and property.[13]

Such individual parishes, however, and other lesser corporations in the Church derive their juridical personality in consequence of a provision of law or through a special concession from a competent ecclesiastical superior, provided that this be given by way of a formal decree and that the purpose of the corporation be religious or charitable.[14]

[11] John A. Abbo and Jerome D. Hannan, *The Sacred Canons* (2 vols., St. Louis: B. Herder Book Co., 1952), II, 705.

[12] *Bradshaw v. Tasken*, 2 My. & K. 221 (1834); *West v. Shuttleworth* 2 My. & K. 684 (1835). Cf. *supra*, p. 13.

[13] Eusebius, *Historia Ecclesiae*, X. 5—Migne, *Patrologiae Cursus Completus, Series Graeca*, (162 vols., Paris, 1857-66), XX, 883 (hereafter cited *MPG*).

[14] Canon 100, § 1.

They derive their origin from ecclesiastical, not divine, law. As these lesser corporations receive their authority to acquire, hold and administer goods from the supreme ecclesiastical authority in the Church, viz. from the Roman Pontiff, it follows that this latter is the principal dispenser, but not the owner or the possessor of ecclesiastical goods. The present law accords with the view expressed by St. Thomas.[15]

In Australia the method by which parish property is held is by a corporation aggregate. The earliest relevant decree is from the I Plenary Council of Australia in 1885, wherein it was enacted that the titles and instruments relating to ecclesiastical goods are to be held by a trusteeship in the name of at least three guardians or trustees to be designated by the ordinary. Among these were to be the bishop himself and at least two priests.[16] The holding of ecclesiastical property in fee simple was fortunately rarely the practice. The successive Plenary Councils of 1895, 1905 and 1937 have but re-enacted the 1885 law.

In operation the corporation aggregate is accepted by the laws of every State, and it functions similarly to the plan acceptable under the laws of the State of New York in the United States of America. Under the New York plan the parish corporation consists of the bishop, the vicar general and the pastor, with two laymen chosen annually by the ecclesiastical authorities. These are authorized to file an incorporating certificate with the Secretary of State. The courts have interpreted the statute as effecting, when its requirements are met, the incorporation of the members of the parish. Under the statute it is further provided that no act of the corporation is valid without the sanction of the bishop or, in his absence or inability to act, of the vicar general, or of the administrator of the diocese. An amendment was enacted in 1902 to permit the bishop to transfer without consideration the property of a divided parish to

[15] Cf. *Summa Theologica,* IIa IIae, q. 100, art. 1, ad 7.

[16] *Acta et Decreta Concilii Plenarii Australiasiae* (Sydney: F. Cunninghame & Co., 1887), p. 91

the parish newly established by the division and to divide the receipts accordingly.[17]

The right of the Church to exact the means of its support, as enunciated in canon 1496, is a natural concomitant to its right as a perfect and sovereign society to acquire temporal goods. "The Church also has the right, independently of the civil power, to demand from the faithful whatever is necessary for the observance of divine worship, for the fitting support of its clerics and other ministers, and the other purposes for which it has been established."[18] The principal means of acquiring ecclesiastical goods and property at the present day are through collections, alms, special fees, charitable subsidy, the cathedraticum, prescription, adverse possession, grants, bequests and last wills. Custom has contributed not a little to the method of acquiring the necessary means for the Church to carry on its end. The Church's insistence on the exercise of this right has usually been in proportion to the generosity of the faithful. While tithes and first fruits were the principal means of support in former centuries, it seems that nowadays the generosity of the faithful is more readily secured by way of appeal and counsel than by way of strict command.[19]

The decrees of the IV Plenary of Australia (1937) concerning ecclesiastical goods, which for the most part merely repeat the decrees of the three former Plenary Councils, contain nothing by way of command or even of exhortation about rendering support to the Church or fitting sustenance to the clergy. But because of the poverty of the faithful generally around the middle of the nineteenth century and the consequent indigence of the Church, the decree *"De Sustentatione Episcoporum et Cleri"* of the II Provincial

[17] Consolidated laws of New York, Art. 5, §§ 90-92. In some states which authorise similar plans, a diocesan corporation can be formed by a substituting of the chancellor in the place held by the bishop. Abbo-Hannan, *The Sacred Canons*, II, 707.

[18] *Canon* 1496.

[19] Vermeersch-Creusen, *Epitome Iuris Canonici* (2 ed., 3 vols., Brugis, 1923-1925), II, n. 87 (hereafter cited *Epitome*).

Council (1869) did contain an exhortation to the bishops to remind the faithful of their obligation in this matter.

> Cum in huius Provinciae diocesibus, paucis exceptis, redditus nulli suppetant praeter oblationes fidelium, quibus Episcopi et clerus sustentetur et variis religionis et pauperum necessitatibus subveniatur, et cum praeterea non pauci inveniantur, qui huiusmodi oblationes, etiam quae debita dici solent (anglice *dues*) quia Deo debentur, solvere negligant, Episcopos hortamur ut fidelibus sibi commissis exponendam curent multiplicem qua adstringamur obligationem, bonorum quae Dominus ipsis largitus est congruam partem erga sacri cultus ministerium retribuere.[20]

Following the distinctions of Roman Law, canon 1497 divides ecclesiastical goods into corporeal, both movable and immovable, and incorporeal. "Temporal property, both movable and immovable corporeal property and incorporeal property, whether it belongs to the Universal Church and the Apostolic See or to some other moral person in the Church, is ecclesiastical property."[21]

The Romans classified things as corporeal or incorporeal in so far as they could be perceived by the senses or not. "Corporales eae sunt, quae sui natura tangi possunt; veluti fundus. . . . Incorporales autem sunt, quae tangi non possunt."[22] Corporeal goods are those that can be perceived by the senses, e.g., land, houses or furniture. Similarly, incorporeal goods are what cannot be perceived by the senses. They consist chiefly of rights to corporeal property, inclusive of claims to it at law. All property, whether corporeal or incorporeal, is called ecclesiastical whenever it belongs to the Universal Church, to the Holy See, or even to some corporation in the Church.[23] The terms "movable" and "immovable goods" are self-explanatory.

[20] *Secundum Concilium Provinciale Australiense, 1869,* sec. 1, p. 89.

[21] Canon 1497, § 1.

[22] *Digesta,* quae recognovit Th. Mommsen, et retractavit P. Krueger (ed. stereotypa 15., Berolini: Apud Weidmonnis 1928), 8, 1, 14pr.

[23] J., D'Annible, *Summula Theologiae Moralis* (3. ed., 3 vols., Romae, 1891), III, n. 77.

Temporal goods are called *sacred,* when by consecration or blessing they are destined for divine worship; *precious,* when their value is notable because of their artistic quality, or their historical importance, or the material of which they are made.[24] The criterion of a *res sacra* in Roman Law was its purpose. Namely, temples and altars consecrated to the gods were considered *"res sacrae."* If they belonged to the deities they were *"res divini iuris"* and were incapable of valuation, mortgage, usucaption or adaption to profane use.[25] The criterion of a *res sacra* in Canon Law and its consequent immunity from profane use is consecration or blessing. For the consecration of anything an episcopal power is necessary unless other provision be made with a special permission granted in the law or by way of special indult.[26] Thus churches, altars, chalices and patens receive a consecration, while sacred vestments, statues, cemeteries, etc., receive a blessing. All blessings, except for special reservations, may be imparted by priests.[27] Even deacons and lectors may in some cases be authorized to bestow these blessings.[28] Theologians and canonists are by no means in agreement as to the postulated worth of value of an article before it is constituted as "precious." It seems that the wording of the canon itself is the most reliable criterion. Namely, if the article has such historical, artistic or intrinsic value as to be worthy of the name "precious" in the accepted use of that word, being thus constituted as an object of singular value, then it would fall into that category. Because of the fluctuation of currency and monetary values in almost every country the pre-Code and pre-war monetary estimate of *"notabilis valor"* has had to be drastically revised. Since the values of the franc and of the lira have dropped to absurb levels and inasmuch as the only relative-

[24] Canon 1497, § 2.

[25] C. P. Sherman, *Roman Law* (2. ed., 3 vols., New Haven, 1922), II, 559.

[26] Canon 1147, § 1.

[27] Canon 1147, § 2, § 3.

[28] Canon 1147, § 4.

ly stable currencies at the time of writing are the American dollar and the pound sterling, it seems that the most reasonable interpretation of *"notable value"* is about $250.00 or 100 pounds sterling. Analogous to the category of precious objects is that of votive offerings made at a shrine or an altar,[29] and major (*insignes*) relics of the saints.[30]

Lest confusion arise in the interpretation of the following canons concerning ecclesiastical goods, an extension of the term "Church" is given in canon 1498. "In the canons that follow, by the term "Church" there is signified not only the Universal Church or the Apostolic See, but also every moral person in the Church, unless from the context of the passage or the nature of the subject matter it is clear that this is not meant."[31]

Article 2. Tenure of Property Acquired by Church Corporations

Canons 1499, 1500 and 1501 deal with the acquisition of property by the Church as a corporation, whether it be by the Universal Church or by an individual church, as expressed in canon 1498. "The Church can acquire temporal goods by all just means which are sanctioned in the case of others by the natural or the positive law."[32] Just as in civil law individual citizens and legally established societies or corporations may acquire and hold title to property, so does the Church in general and as an individual corporation possess goods.

From the context of the canon it is clear that the property rights of legal ecclesiastical persons are dealt with. Whatever an individual person in the Church, e.g., a bishop or a priest, holds in his own right he holds in the same manner as any other citizen. His personal savings, no matter

[29] Cf. S.C.C., resp., 14 ian. 1922 (*AAS*, XIV [1922], 160); Bouscaren, *Canon Law Digest.* I, 730.

[30] Cf. S.C.C., resol., 13 iul. 1919 (*AAS*, XI, [1919], 416); Bouscaren, *op. cit.*, I. 729.

[31] Canon 1498.

[32] Canon 1499, § 1.

from whatever source they accrue, are held in his own right. They are not, therefore, ecclesiastical goods. The right of a corporation to acquire property is based on the same reasons which justify the acquisition of property by an individual. Every state recognizes, or should recognize, the individual's right to own property.[33]

The Church acts like other corporations, in strict accord with justice when it uses the means that are sanctioned by the natural and the positive law for the acquisition of goods. Besides outright purchase, such traditional means as donations, taxes, tithes, first fruits, pious foundations, legacies, last wills, prescription and adverse possession can serve this purpose.[34]

The second paragraph of canon 1499 declares that the ownership of property resides in that juridical person which has legitimately acquired it. That is to say the exclusive ownership belongs to whatever particular church or juridical entity in the Church has acquired the goods. The Code in thus legislating confirms the teaching of the Council of Trent,[35] and the opinion of many eminent theologians and canonists.[36] Thus also did the III Plenary Council of Baltimore (1884) decree: "The corporation that acquires the property enjoys the ownership of that property under the jurisdiction of the Holy See."[37]

In virtue of his position as supreme dispenser of all ecclesiastical property, the Roman Pontiff enjoys a right analogous to the right of eminent domain in reference to the property of subordinate ecclesiastical bodies. Because of this power he can condone usurpations by the secular

[33] Leo XIII, litt. encycl. *Immortale Dei* 1 nov. 1885—*Fontes*, n. 592; Leo XIII. litt. encycl. *Rerum novarum*, 15 maii 1891—*Fontes*, n. 611.

[34] *Acta et Decreta Concilii Plenarii Americae Latinae* (Romae, 1900), n. 826.

[35] Sess. XIV, *de ref.*, c. 9; Sess. XXV, *de regular.*, c. 3.

[36] Cf. *Summa Theologica*, IIa IIae, q. 100, a. 1, ad 7: D'Annibale, *op. cit.*, I, n. 43, and III, n. 77; J. Laurentius, *Institutiones Iuris Ecclesiastici* (Friburgi Brisgoviae, 1908), p. 635; Wernz-Vidal, *Ius Canonicum*, III, 139.

[37] *III Conc. Plen. Baltimor.*, n. 264.

authority of the property of these subordinate ecclesiastical bodies, or transfer the property of one of them to another. In doing so, however, he is required to observe the conditions that obtain in the case of the exercise of the right of eminent domain on the part of the secular power, i.e., he must be moved by a serious reason and must provide for an adequate compensation.

No others in the Church enjoy this power over the subordinate bodies subject to their jurisdiction. Superiors General of religious communities cannot transfer the property of one province to another, and bishops cannot transfer the property of one parish to another, no matter how serious a reason there may be for doing so, even though they may be willing to provide adequate compensation. Even should the civil law recognize such an act on the bishop's part, as it would if it had granted him incorporation as a corporation sole, his act, if unauthorized by apostolic indult, would be canonically invalid and unjust.[38]

To insure stability, to safeguard the property and to prevent ecclesiastical goods from falling into alien hands it is essential that all titles and instruments be drawn up according to the civil laws of the country in which the property is held. As in America so in Australia the legal device by which a corporation holds property may be by a corporation aggregate or a corporation sole. The forced adoption of the method whereby a church held property in fee simple was fortunately only rarely the practice and has now largely fallen into desuetude.

The method of holding in fee simple meant that the bishop or the pastor held and administered church property in his own name and by an absolute and full legal title. Even though this form was resorted to only when safer and more convenient means were prohibited by state laws, nevertheless the experience of more than half a century proved that

[38] Abbo-Hannan, *The Sacred Canons*, II, 711. Cf. also Vermeersch-Creusen,*Epitome,* II, n. 821; A. De Meester, *Juris Canonici et Juris Canonico-Civilis Compendium* (3 vols. in 4, Brugis; Desclée, 1921-28), III, n. 1449 ,hereafter cited *Compendium*).

it was not a feasible method, but rather a highly dangerous one.[39] Property held in fee simple was subject to taxation, death duties and inheritance taxes. In the event of bankruptcy the entire church property of a diocese could be assigned to creditors. Furthermore, the bishop himself was liable for all debts of the various parishes.

In addition, during the interim between the death of a bishop and a pastor and the appointment of his successor the resultant confusion could very easily jeopardize the property holdings of the diocese or the parish. It could happen, too, that the deceased bishop's or pastor's last will and testament would be disputed, with the consequent passing of consecrated and blessed objects as well as valuable land and buildings into alien hands. Hence it is not to be wondered at that in 1840 the Sacred Congregation for the Propagation of the Faith drew up regulations and suggestions for the safeguarding of ecclesiastical goods held in fee simple.[40]

Likewise the first three Plenary Councils of Australia admonished bishops and pastors to exercise care lest ecclesiastical goods be expropriated wherever and whenever they were held in fee simple.

> Ad evitandas lites quae, cum scandalo fidelium et bonorum ecclesiasticorum iactura, possint post eorum mortem oriri de bonis quae ab episcopis et a sacerdotibus tenentur: praecipimus ut singuli episcopi et sacerdotes omnes bonorum ecclesiasticorum possessionem aut administrationem quocumque modo habentes, testamenta sua post tres menses rite conficiant et signent et eadem in loco tuto ab episcopo designato reposita habeant.[41]

In 1911 the Sacred Congregation of the Council outlined

[39] William J. Doheny, *Church Property: Modes of Acquisition*, The Catholic University of America Studies in Canon and Roman Law, No. 41 (Washington, D.C.: The Catholic University of America, 1927), p. 41.

[40] S.C. de Prop. Fide, decr. 15 dec. 1840—*Collectanea Sacrae Congregationis de Propagonda Fide* (2 vols., Romae: Typographia Polyglotta, 1907), n. 916 (hereafter cited *Coll. S.C.P.F.*).

[41] *Acta et Decreta Conc. Plen. Aust. II*, decr. 342, p. 120.

the preferable means to be used, viz., the parish corporation, and ordered the abolition of the method of holding church property in fee simple.

> Ex methodis quae pro possidendis et administrando ecclesiasticis bonis nunc vigent in Statibus Americae Foederatis ea ceteris praeferenda est, quae vulgo dicitur *Parish corporation,* cum illis tamen conditionibus et cautelis, quibus in statu Neo-Eboracensi in usu est.[42] Hanc igitur methodum episcopi, si lex civilis consentiat, quoad bona temporalia in suam diocesim introducere statim curabunt. Si vero lex non consentiat, apud civiles auctoritates efficaciter instabunt ut quam primum concedatur.
>
> In locis tantum in quibus a lege civili non admittitur *Parish corporation* et donec eius concessio obtineri nequeat, permittitur alia methodus quae dici solet *Corporation sole,* ita tamen ut episcopus in administratione bonorum ecclesiasticorum procedat, auditis interesse habentibus et con sultoribus diocesanis, et in negotiis maioris momenti de eorum consensu, super hoc ipsius episcopi conscientia onerata.
>
> Methodus quem vocant in *Fee Simple* omnino est abolenda.[43]

Lest any vestige of the fee simple idea remain in the minds of administrators of church property the IV Plenary Council of Australia (1937) added several decrees absolutely forbidding priests to hold ecclesiastical goods in their own name or in their own right. It further specified that every class of ecclesiastical goods, church, school, rectory, buildings, land, trust funds or money itself, belongs to the church.

> It is unlawful for any priest, without the written permission of the ordinary, to hold in his own name and in his own right the church, school, rectory, parochial or cemetery funds or any ecclesiastical goods whatsoever towards which the faithful have contributed in any way, but must trans-

[42] Cf. *supra,* p. 23.

[43] *Periodica,* VI, (1912), 101; *Ecclesiastical Review,* XLV (1911), 585. Cf. Doheny, *op. cit.,* p. 41.

> fer them as soon as possible to the ordinary or to a corporate body sanctioned by him.[44]
>
> Likewise we strictly forbid a pastor or any priest to deposit money belonging to the church in his own name, or to have the bank book in the name of his own private person, but he must place it in the name of the trustees, of whom mention is made in decree no. 655.[45]

So strict is the law in this matter that the Council invoked a *ferendae sententiae* penal sanction, against all violators.

> If a pastor and other administrators of ecclesiastical goods, contrary to the prescriptions of the preceding decree, retain church money or ecclesiastical goods along with their own property, or in their own name, or bank it in their own name, or permit the bank books to be kept in the name of their own private persons, they shall be punished by the ordinary, even to the point of suspension or of complete removal from office within the ordinary's prudential option.[46]

It is significant that, after the decree of the Sacred Congregation of the Council on 1911, even though it was intended specifically for the United States of America, the decree concerning fee simple tenure of ecclesiastical property was deleted from the IV Plenary Council in 1937. In any case it was no longer necessary, since all the states of Australia recognize the holding of property under the corporate system. The corporation aggregate rather than the corporation sole is the more desirable system mentioned in all the four Plenary Councils of Australia.[47]

The corporation sole is a legal entity consisting of one person at a time. When that person dies the fee is held in abeyance until a successor is elected. Upon his election

[44] *Conc. Plen. IV Aust. et Novae Zelandiae, 1937,* decr. n. 673, p. 121.

[45] *Ibid.,* decr. n. 674.

[46] *Ibid.,* decr. n. 675. Cf. canons 2195, 2222, § 1.

[47] Concil. Plen. Aust. I, 1885, decr. n. 271, p. 91; Concil. Plen. Aust. II, 1895, decr. n. 341, p. 119; Concil. Plen. Aust. III, 1905, decr. n. 368, p. 126; Concil. Plen. Aust. IV, 1937, decr. n. 655' p. 118.

to the office the successor assumes all the duties and privileges which the aims and ends of the established corporation direct. This was the system of property ownership that was resorted to by many dioceses in the United States of America in an effort to liberate property from the control of trustees when the system of lay trusteeism became a menace. It was also more desirable since it concentrated the management of temporal affairs in the hands of the bishops.[48] In some states, however, the corporation sole was not recognized by law, inasmuch as the legislators believed that it was an undue privilege for the Church, which was considered the principal beneficiary of such a law.[49]

Article 3. The Corporation Aggregate

The third means of holding church property is the corporation aggregate. Under this system, as the name suggests, the property is vested in a body corporate formed from a group of members of the society or church. The incorporators hold the property under their control, but their possession is the possession of the artificial person, whose agents they are. They manage and administer the property, but this right is an authority and not an estate or title. In many respects their direction and discretion are similar to that vested in the board of directors in any other corporation.

This is the method preferred by the Sacred Congregation of the Council in the 1911 Decree.[50] It is also the system envisaged in all four Plenary Councils of Australia. The relevant decree in the IV Plenary Council completely omits the earlier added phrase, "where other provision is not made by the civil law," so that it reads as follows:

> To prevent ecclesiastical goods from falling into the hands of others, the bishop will take care that title deeds and instruments be drawn up in the name of at least three guardians nominated by the

[48] Doheny, *op. cit.*, p. 39.

[49] *Union Church* v. *Sanders*, 1 Houst. (Del.), 100; 63 Am. Dec. 187.

[50] *Supra*, p. 31.

> ordinary of the place. Among these will be the bishop of the diocese and at least two priests prudent and skilled in matters of this kind. These must meet once a year to watch over the security of the property. If any one of these had been removed for any cause, the bishop must appoint another in his place.[51]

On July 4, 1936, the State of New South Wales assented to the "*Roman Catholic Church Trust Property Act, 1936.*" This provided the IV Plenary Council, when held the following year, with the opportunity of legislating in accordance with the acceptable provisions of the new act. After an introductory preamble, sections 1 and 2 state the title of the act and define for the purposes of the act the ecclesiastical terminology used.

> "*Bishop*" means the person for the time being administering a diocese, whether as Archbishop or Bishop, Co-adjutor Archbishop or Co-adjutor Bishop, Vicar Capitular or Administrator.
> "*Church*" means the Roman Catholic Church.
> "*Church Trust Property*" means land situated in New South Wales, for the time being subject to any trust created before or after the commencement of this act, for the Church or for the use or benefit or for any purpose of the Church, including the land the subject of the provisions of St. Patrick's College (Manly) Act, 1914, but does not include land held on any trust, created before or after the commencement of this Act, for any Order or Community of the Church or for any association of members of the Church for the use or benefit of or for any purpose of any such Order, Community or association.[52]

The exception mentioned in the latter section of the act concerns the property of religious orders and communities for whom the "*Roman Catholic Church Communities' Lands Act, 1942-1948,*" defines *Community Land* as "land situated in New South Wales for the time being subject to any trust created before or after the commencement of this Act

[51] *Concil. Plen. Aust. IV*, decr. n. 655, p. 118.
[52] *Roman Catholic Church Trust Property Act, 1936*. sec. 2. p. 2.

for a community, or for the use or benefit or for any purpose of a community, but does not include any land which is church trust property within the meaning of the *Roman Catohlic Church Trust Property Act, 1936*."[53]

> "*Diocese*" means a diocese (including an Archdiocese) for the time being of the Church, situated in New South Wales, and whether created before or after the commencement of this Act.
>
> "*Diocesan Consultors*" means the Diocesan Consultors for the time being of a diocese, or in relation to a diocese in which a Cathedral Chapter shall for the time being exist, the members for the time being of that Cathedral Chapter.
>
> "*Land*" includes tenements and hereditaments, corporeal and incorporeal, and every estate and interest therein whether vested or contingent, freehold or leasehold, and whether at law or in equity.[54]

Sections 3 and 4 of the Act establish the personnel of the trusteeship, namely, that in effect they should be priests of the diocese, and the method of incorporation, namely, corporation aggregate, as stated in all four plenary councils.

> There shall be for each diocese trustees of Church trust property, who shall be the Bishop of the diocese and the Diocesan Consultors of the diocese.
>
> The trustees of Church trust property for each diocese shall, by virtue of this Act, be a body corporate, having pertpetual succession and a common seal, and being capable of acquiring, holding and disposing of any property, real or personal, and of suing and being sued in its corporate name, and of doing and suffering all such acts and things as bodies corporate may by law do or suffer: Provided that this subsection shall not operate to incorporate the trustees of Church trust property in any diocese created after the commencement of this Act until the publication in the Gazette of the notification required by section five of this Act.
>
> 2. The corporate names of the trustees of Church trust property for the several dioceses existing

[53] *Roman Catholic Church Communities' Lands Act, 1942-1948*, sec. 2, p. 3.

[54] *Roman Catholic Church Trust Property Act, 1936*, sec. 2, p. 3.

> at the commencement of this Act shall be—for the Archdiocese of Sydney, the trustees of the Roman Catholic Church for the Archdiocese of Sydney:[55]

The Act then lists the existing dioceses in the State of New South Wales in alphabetical order, namely Armidale, Bathurst, Goulburn, Lismore, Maitland, Wagga Wagga and Wilcannia-Forbes.

Section 5 of the Act deals with the creation of the new trusteeship when new dioceses are established.

> 1. Upon the creation of a diocese after the commencement of this Act, the Bishop of the diocese so created and the Bishop of any diocese out of which the diocese is so created shall, by notification signed by them and published in the Gazette, announce the creation of the diocese, and its name and the corporate name of the trustees of the Church trust property for the diocese.
>
> 2. A printed paper purporting to be a copy of the Gazette, and to have been printed by the Government Printer, and containing what purports to be a copy of a notification published pursuant to subsection one of this section shall be conclusive evidence of the statements so published.
>
> 3. A diocese shall not be extinguished by the creation wholly or partly thereout of a new diocese or by any other alteration of its boundaries.[56]

Section 6 of the Act deals with the seal and quorum, as does decree 655 of the IV Plenary Council.

> The members of the time being of each corporate body created by this Act shall have the custody of the common seal, and the form of such seal and all other matters relating thereto shall, subject as in this section mentioned, be from time to time, determined at a meeting of the body corporate.
>
> The Bishop and two other members of each such body corporate shall constitute a quorum for the purpose of any meeting of the body corporate.
>
> Every meeting of the body corporate at which

[55] *Roman Catholic Church Trust Property Act, 1936*, sec. 3, sec. 4, p. 3.

[56] *Ibid.*, sec. 5. p. 4.

> a quorum is present shall be competent to transact any business of the body corporate.
>
> The common seal of any such body corporate shall not be affixed to any instrument except in pursuance of a resolution passed at a meeting of the body corporate.
>
> Every instrument to which the common seal is so affixed shall be signed by the Bishop who is a member of the body corporate and by two other members of the body corporate.[57]

Decree 655 of the IV Plenary Council obliges the bishop always to maintain the necessary quorum. "If any one of these had been removed for any cause, the bishop must appoint another in his place." While section 7 (2) of the Act suspends the powers and capacity of the corporation to operate unless a duly constituted quorum, the bishop and two other members, is present, nevertheless, its capacity and powers are unaffected if other vacancies in the membership of the body corporate occur.

> 1. Except as in this section mentioned, no capacity or power of a body corporate created by this Act shall be affected by the existence of vacancies in its membership.
>
> 2. Where for any reason a quorum of a body corporate created by this Act cannot be constituted all powers exercisable by the body corporate and its capacity for doing any act or thing shall be suspended, but shall, by virtue of this Act, revive as soon as a quorum of such body corporate is capable of being constituted.[58]

Section 8 of the *Roman Catholic Church Trust Property Act, 1936,* treats of the vesting of Church trust property.

> 1. All Church trust property which at the time of creation of any body corporate by this Act is situated within the diocese for which the body corporate is created by virtue of this Act;
>
> (a) vest in that body corporate upon its creation; and
>
> (b) be thereupon divested from the person in

[57] *Ibid.,* sec. 6. p. 5, 6.

[58] *Ibid.,* sec. 7, p. 5.

> whom it was vested before the creation of such body corporate.
>
> 2. No vesting by virtue of this Act shall affect any encumbrance, lien, estate or interest to which, at the time of the vesting, the property so vested was subject in the hands of the person from whom it was divested.
>
> The body corporate in which the property vests shall become (liable) jointly with the person liable at the time of the vesting and, severally, liable under every contract, engagement and cause of action, in relation to the property vested, under which the person from whom the property was divested was liable at the time of the vesting.
>
> The body corporate shall be liable to indemnify the person from whom the property was divested, his executors and administrators against every claim, action, suit and any other proceeding which shall be made or taken in respect of any such contract, engagement or cause of action.
>
> The person from whom the property was divested shall have a charge or lien on the property divested to the extent to which and in the circumstances in which the charge or lien would have attached if the property had not been divested; but the charge or lien, or possibility thereof, shall, in favour of a person dealing for value with the body corporate in which the property is vested, be deemed to have been extinguished unless the person entitled thereto has within a period of six months after the commencement of this Act given written notice to the body corporate of its existence or of the possibility of its arising.
>
> A statement under the common seal of the body corporate that no such notice has been received within such period shall be conclusive evidence of the fact so stated in favour of any person dealing for value with the body corporate in respect of the divested property.

The powers of the Catholic Church Trust are outlined in section 9 of the Act.

> Every body corporate created by this Act shall have power, from time to time—
>
> (a) to purchase, take on lease, or acquire by gift,

devise, bequest, exchange or otherwise any real or personal property; and

(b) in relation to any Church trust property at any time vested in it—

(i) to sell it, and to exchange it for other land, and to transfer or convey Church trust property so sold or exchanged to the purchaser or person taking in exchange, freed and discharged from all trusts affecting the same in the hands of the body corporate; and

(ii) to demise or let it for such term at such rent and with or without taking a premium, fine or foregift and subject to such provisions as to the body corporate shall appear desirable; and

(iii) to accept surrender of leases, upon such terms and subject to such conditions as to the body corporate shall appear desirable; and

(iv) to raise money on the security of it on such terms and conditions as to the body corporate shall appear desirable; and

(v) to declare trusts of it or any estate or interest in it created by the body corporate for any Order or Community of the Church or for any association of members of the Church or for the use or benefit of or for any purpose of any such Order, Community or association, and to which trusts are so declared, or to either to retain the property in relation vest it, or any estate or interest so created, in other trustees upon the trusts so declared; and

(c) for any purpose mentioned in this section to execute all such instruments as to the body shall appear proper.[59]

Every instrument bearing what purports to be the common seal of a body corporate created by this Act for any diocese created before or after the commencement of this Act, and purporting to be signed by the Bishop of that diocese and two other members of that body corporate shall, in

[59] *Roman Catholic Church Trust Property Act, 1936*, sec. 9, p. 6, 7.

> favour of every person claiming, for value and in good faith, under or through that instrument, be conclusively presumed to have been duly executed by the body corporate the common seal of which it purports to bear.[60]

As with every other juridical entity or corporation, the rights of those dealing with them have to be considered; so do sections 11 and 12 of the *Roman Catholic Church Trust Property, 1936,* outline protective measures affecting purchasers of property from such bodies corporate.[61]

Section 13 dealing with the preservation of trusts is similar in content to section 2 of canon 1499; namely, the ownership of property, under the supreme authority of the Apostolic See, belongs to that moral person which lawfully acquired it.[62]

> All Church trust property for the time being vested in a body corporate by this Act shall be held by it on the trusts, if any, expressly declared, on trust for the Church in the diocese for which the body corporate exists. Provided, however, that the powers conferred by section nine of this Act shall be exercisable in relation to all Church trust property notwithstanding any trust or provision affecting it in the hands of the body corporate.[63]
>
> All grants of land hitherto made by the canon are held to be valid[64] and *The Roman Catholic Diocese of Lismore Church Lands Act, 1908,* and *St. Patrick's College (Manly) Act, 1914,* are repealed.[65]
>
> 14. No title to any land granted by the Crown before the commencement of this Act, for or for the use, benefit or purposes of the Church shall be held bad, either at law or in equity, by reason of any breach or non-performance, before or after the commencement of this Act, of any condition,

[60] *Ibid.*, sec. 10, p. 7.

[61] *Ibid.*, *cf.* sec. 11, 12, pp. 8 ff.

[62] Cf. Canon 1499, § 2.

[63] *Roman Catholic Church Trust Property Act, 1936*, sec. 13, p. 10.

[64] *Ibid.*, sec. 14.

[65] *Ibid.*, sec. 15.

trust or proviso contained in the grant by the Crown of the land, and every provision for forfeiture or reverter in respect of any such breach or non-performance shall be deemed to have been released by the Crown as the date of the Crown grant.

15. (1) The Roman Catholic Diocese of Lismore Church Lands Act, 1908, and St. Patrick's College (Manly) Act, 1914, are hereby repealed, but neither of those repeals shall affect—

(a) any right accrued or obligation incurred before the commencement of this Act, or

(b) the validity or invalidity or any operation, effect or consequence of any instrument executed or made or anything done or suffered before the commencement of this Act; or

(c) any action, proceeding or thing, at the commemcement of this Act, pending or uncompleted.

(2) Every such action, proceeding and thing may be carried on and completed as if the Acts hereby repealed remained in force.

(3) Nothing in this section shall limit any saving in the *Interpretation* Act of 1897.

Thus church property is amply safeguarded from the dangers of the fee simple method, for the death of a trustee does not affect the life of the corporation. It allows the Catholic laymen on the board of trustees a voice in the administration, but at the same time retain for the clergy, *"episcopus et ad minus duo sacerdotes,"* the controlling power in the management of the property.

As the Church grows and its integrated corporations increase, it becomes necessary or at least expedient to divide it and to establish similar juridical entities from the divided portions. Thus are parishes separated and certain territories apportioned to them. Like any business venture, the making of a new parish is fraught with many difficulties, not the least of which is the need of capital and finances firmly to establish it.

When the division of a parish has been made[66] it is the

[66] Cf. canon 216.

duty of the competent ecclesiastical authority to distribute the resources equitably.[67] When the territory of a legal ecclesiastical person is divided, so that either a part of it is united to another legal person, or a new and distinct legal person is created for the separated territory, the common goods which were destined for the benefit of the entire territory, and also the debts contracted for the whole territory, shall be divided in proper proportion and in all fairness by the competent ecclesiastical authority which orders the division. The intentions of the founders and benefactors, the acquired legal rights, and the special laws governing legal persons must be respected.[68]

In dividing a parish the ordinary must assign an adequate income to the newly erected perpetual vicarage or parish, with the due observance of the provisions of canon 1500. Unless this income can be found elsewhere, it must be taken from the income derived in any way by the mother church, provided a sufficient income is left to the mother church.[69] In virtue of canon 1500 a proportionate division of the common property of the parish is authorized in a division or a dismemberment of it. This apportionment in addition to the property or the revenue that is accessory to the specific dissevered territory, yields to the new parish. The capital, however, of specific endowments set up for the mother parish cannot be diverted to the new parish. This is also true of the income derived from them.[70]

Whenever an ecclesiastical corporation owning property becomes extinct, then its property must attach to some other moral person in the Church. A corporation becomes extinct in two ways, namely, through suppression by the legitimate ecclesiastical authority or through the non-manifes-

[67] Reg. 55, R. J., in VI° "Qui sentit onus, sentite debet commodum, et e contra." Cf. also canons 1427, and 1500.

[68] Canon 1500. Cf. also canon 1427.

[69] Canon 1427, § 3. C. 3, X, *de ecclesiis aedificandis vel reparandis*, III, 48; Conc. Trident., sess. XXI, *de ref.*, c. 4.

[70] Abbo-Hannan, *The Sacred Canons*, II, 660.

tation of any and legal vitality for the space of one hundred years.[71] Canon 1501 legislates for these two contingencies. When an ecclesiastical legal person has become extinct, the ownership of its property attaches to the immediately higher ecclesiastical moral person, provided, however, that there be always respected the intentions of the founders or the donors, all legally vested rights, and also such special laws as governed the legal person which has ceased to be.[72]

[71] Canon 102, § 1.
[72] Canon 1501.

CHAPTER III

METHODS OF ACQUIRING INCOME AND PROPERTY

ARTICLE 1. TITHES AND FIRST FRUITS

The oldest and best known means by which the Church acquires income are stated in canon 1502. "The payment of tithes and first fruits shall be governed according to the special laws and laudable customs of each country."[1] *Decimae* or tithes are a tenth part of the fruits or profits justly acquired and due to God in recognition of his supreme dominion over men, while *primitiae* are the first fruits of fields, gardens, orchards, etc., or the first offspring of animals. Tithes and first fruits were of strict precept among the Jews in virtue of the Old Testament ordinances.[2] Hence it was but a logical step for the first Christians, mostly converts from Judaism, to introduce a similar practice in the early Christian communities.[3] Such a system has been the practice in the Church far almost the whole period of its history. A sub-Apostolic Collection of Ordinances[4] and the early Fathers, St. Irenaeus, Origen and St. Augustine,[5] all mention tithes as a means for supporting the ministers of the Church and alleviating the needs of the poor. Gregory VII (1073-1085) in condemning those who refused to pay tithes stated that they incurred the danger of eternal damnation.[6] Almost five centuries later the Council of Trent

[1] Canon 1502.

[2] Levit., XXVII; Deuter., XIV: 22; XXIV: 1-11; Exod; XXIII: 16; XXXIV: 22.

[3] As the historical survey of *Decimae* and *Primitiae* is outside the scope of this work, the reader is directed to Chapter IV of Msgr. Doheny's excellent work, *Church Property: Modes of Acquisition*, pp. 44 ff.

[4] F. X. Funk, *Doctrina Duodecim Apostolorum*, Tubingae, 1887, p. 95.

[5] *Adversus Haereses*, IV c. 18, n. 2—*MPG*, VII, 1025; *Homilia IX in Numeros*, n. 2—*MPG*, XII, 644; *In Psalm. CXLVI*, n. 17—*MPL*, XXXVII, 1911.

[6] C. 1, C. XVI, q. 7.

still insisted on their payment.[7] But, since the Council of Trent the various means of church support have been much better organized, and the generosity of the faithful has in general obviated the need for detailed and stringent laws in this regard. At the present time there is no universal law demanding the payment of tithes or of first fruits. The Church insists on their payment only in those countries where such special laws or customs still obtain. In Australia the custom of tithes has never existed, and the pew rent system has long since fallen into disuse. The voluntary offerings of the faithful, seasonal and occasional collections, and the payment of dues in connection with the performance or ministration of various functions have generally proved sufficient in care of the Church's needs.

Canon 1503 seeks to correct many abuses that solicitors of alms and collectors in general have caused through the centuries. "Without prejudice to canons 621-624, private persons, whether clerics or lay persons, are forbidden to solicit funds for any pious or ecclesiastical institute or purpose without the written permission of the Apostolic See or of both their own ordinary and the local ordinary."[8] Medicant orders strictly so called are by canon 621 freed from this ruling provided they solicit within the confines of the diocese in which their houses are situated. If they seek alms elsewhere they need the written permission of the ordinary of that place.[9]

As canon 1503 states, all private persons are subject to this prohibition. This prohibition, however, does not apply to a pastor in his own parish for there he is acting in his official capacty as *parochus*.[10] Furthermore, wth or without the requisite written permission, the end should always be a pious

[7] Conc. Trident., sess. XXV, *de ref.*, c. 2.

[8] Canon 1503.

[9] Cf. canon 621, § 1. This is to be understood as applying only to religious who are mendicants in the strict sense and not to those who are called such in a broader sense as for example, the Order of Preachers. Cf. *AAS*, 11-478; Bouscaren, *Canon Law Digest*, I, 323.

[10] Cf. canon 415, § 2, 5°.

one. Permission for private persons to collect alms can be obtained in two ways: first, by permission from the Holy see, viz., from the Sacred Congregation of the Council or, for missionary countries, from the Sacred Congregation for the Propagation of the Faith or, in the case of the Oriental Church, from the Sacred Congregation for the Oriental Church. Even when this permission has been obtained the local ordinary can, if there is no executor for the rescript, demand its presentation for recognition and verification.[11] The second way for private persons to collect alms is by way of permission from their own ordinary and the local ordinary. There is nothing in the law with regard to seeking authorization from the local pastor, but courtesy and common sense would surely demand a charitable understanding between the respective interests.

The phrase *"stipem cogere"* points to the practice of collecting from a fairly large number of persons. Hence, if a person were to seek aid from a few personal friends or acquaintenances he would not be soliciting help in violation of the ruling of canon 1503.[12] Authors generally consider this prohibition to apply to personal collection tours, which are frequently indiscreet and importunate in that they can so readily violate parochial rights, rather than to appeals for aid by mail.[13] Augustine, however, held that the Code does not distinguish between personal or oral quest and begging by letters, and that accordingly both forms are prohibited.[14] In view of modern postal facilities and in consequence of the usages engendered by mail order businesses, this latter viewpoint seems certainly to be the better opinion.

Article 2. The Cathedraticum

Canons 1504-1507 deal with the taxation power of local

[11] Cf. canon 51.

[12] D. Pruemmer, *Manuale Iuris Canonici* (3. ed., Frigburgi Brisgoviae, 1922), p. 521.

[13] Vermeersch-Creusen, *Epitome.*

[14] C. Augustine, *The Pastor According to the New Code of Canon Law* (St. Louis, 1923), p. 211.

ordinaries. The *cathedraticum* is a moderate tax which all churches or benefices subject to the episcopal jurisdiction as well as lay confraternities must pay to the bishop annually as a token of their subjection. The cathedraticum has always been a most controversial matter and the bête-noire of certain ecclesiastics for many centuries. All churches and benefices subject to the jurisdiction of a bishop, as well as confraternities of the laity, shall as a sign of their allegiance pay annually to the bishop a cathedratic payment or a moderate tax determined in accordance with the norm of canon 1507, § 1, unless it has already been determined by ancient custom.[15] The cathedraticum which, as the canon states, should be moderate is a token payment, a *signum subjectionis* and is called *cathedraticum* because it is given as a reminder that parish churches are sprung from the cathedral church.[16] Sometimes it was called *"Synodaticum"* because of the occasion on which it was paid, viz, at the annual diocesan synod, and also *"Paschalis,"* when it was exacted at Easter time.[17] The purpose of the cathedraticum is simply the registering of the honor, respect, and subjection that the beneficiary has for the bishop. The very words of the canon suggest that its payment serves not primarily for the increase of the episcopal income but rather as a sign of subjection to the ordinary. Hence the quantity or the amount of this token annual offering is to be *moderate*. Lest bishops err in fixing arbitrarily the amount to be paid, a determined sum should be agreed upon at the provincial council, or at least at a meeting of the bishops of the whole province.[18]

In the early centuries custom rather than law suggested

[15] Canon 1504.

[16] S.C.C., *Aquilina, Cathedratici*, 24. martii, 1906—*Thesaurus Resolutionum Sacrae Congregationis Concilii* (167 vols., Urbini, 1718-1741; Romae 1741-1908), CLXV (1906), 345; AAS, IX (1917), 499.

[17] *AAS*, IX, (1917), 498. Cf. c. 16, X, *de officio iudicis ordinarii*, I, 30; c. 20, X, *de censibus*, III, 39.

[18] Wernz-Vidal, *Ius Canonicum*. Vol. IV, *De Rebus*, Pars II, p. 326. Cf. can. 1507, § 1.

and regulated the payment of the cathedraticum.[19] The earliest extant legislation is found in the III Council of Braga in Spain in the sixth century. This council prescribed that the bishop could not exact more than two *"solidi"* from his churches in payment of the cathedratic tribute.

> Placuit, ut nullus episcoporum, cum per dioeceses suas ambulant, praeter honorem cathedrae suae, id est, duos solidos, aliquid aliud per ecclesias tollat, neque tertiam partem ex quacumque oblatione populi in ecclesiis parochialibus requiret; sed illa tertia pars pro luminariis ecclesiae, vel recuperatione servetur, et singulis annis episcopo inde ratio fiat.[20]

Similar legislation was enacted at the VII Council of Toledo (646)[21] and at the Council of Ravenna (997).[22] In the early twelfth century Pope Gelasius II (1118-1119) urged that the cathedraticum be not extended beyond the customary amount.[23] Alexander III (1159-1181), fifty years later, permitted bishops to exact the cathedraticum[24] and Honorius III (1216-1227) obliged chapels and benefices to its payment.[25]

The Council of Trent made no mention of the cathedraticum, but it did prohibit bishops from exacting a fee while making their diocesan visitation.[26] St. Charles Borromeo, the shining light of the sixteenth century and an authoritative interpreter of the legislation of the Council of Trent,

[19] L. Ferraris, *Bibliotheca Prompta Canonica, Juridica, Moralis, Theologica, necnon Ascetica, Polemica, Rubricistica, Historica,* ed., Migne, (8 vols., Parisiis, 1860-1863), s.v. *Cathedraticum,* Art. 1, n.5.

[20] Conc. Bracarense III (572), can. 2: Joannes Mansi, *Sacrorum Conciliorum Nova et Amplissima Collectio,* (53 vols., Parisiis, 1901-1927), IX, 839 (hereafter cited Ss. Concilia). Wernz-Vidal, *op. cit., loc. cit.*

[21] Can. 4—Ss. Concilia X, 768.

[22] Can. 2—Ss. Concilia XIX, 219.

[23] C. 4, C. X, q. 3.

[24] C. 9, X. *de censibus, exactionibus et procurationibus,* II, 39 .

[25] C. 16, X, *de officio iudicis ordinarii,* I, 31.

[26] Conc. Trident., sess. XXIV, *de ref.,* c. 3.

re-enacted the law of the cathedraticum in the II Provincial Council of Milan (1568):

> Illud sacris Canonibus constitutum est, ut a singulis parochis dioecesana Synodo cathedratici nomine solidi duo exigantur; idque argumento honoris, qui cathedrali ecclesiae tanquam matri a caeteris parochialibus Ecclesiis tribui debetur nos tamen hanc pecuniae summulam, quae superioribus temporibus huic Metropolitanae Ecclesiae eo nomine debita est, nec persoluta tamen, eam omnem etsi iure nostro exigere poteramus, quoniam quod eo nomine solvi debet praescribi non potest, remittimus ac condonamus iis ipsis parochis, qui hoc ipsum cathedraticum praestare debebant. Sed ut in omni re Metropolitanae nostrae Ecclesiae dignitatem et ius retineamus, et quantum in nobis est, conservemus; illud universos et singulos parochos monemus, ut reliquis quae Deo dante in posterum quotannis habentur Synodis dioecesanis, hos ipsos duos solidos, quos honoris erga se Metropolitanae Ecclesiae iure debere sciunt, omnino persolvant.[27]

In the payment of the cathedraticum it seems that the point at issue in every century was not so much the bishop's prerogative in the matter but rather the amount that should be paid. From earliest times the amount was set at two *solidi,* and this amount was uniformly insisted on in later legislation.[28] The cathedraticum was of set purpose to be kept low and equal for all churches and benefices. The Church's intention has always been that it is not an income-producing measure, or a means of support for the bishop, proportionate to the wealth and size of the parishes and other benefices subject to him, but rather a token rendering of the honour, respect and subjection due him.

This very point was insisted on in a decision of the Sacred Congregation of the Council of 1920. Therein it was decided that no tax should be levied upon confraternities

[27] Decretum XLI, *Acta Ecclesiae Mediolanensis* (Mediolani, 1599), p. 364. Cf. S.C.C., *Civitatis Castelli et Altrina,* 20 aug. 1917—*AAS,* IX, (1917), 499.

[28] Cf. *Conc. Bracarense III, supra.* Decretum XLI, *Acta Ecclesiae Mediolanensis, supra.*

and parishes in proportion to the number of their members. The Sacred Congregation further confirmed its decision on the ground that any such proportionate and *pro rata* system of taxation exceeds the limits of moderation prescribed by law and tradition in the Church, and destroys the essentially honorific character of the cathedraticum by equivalently rendering it a purely fiscal exaction ill in accord with the ancient canonical concept of this tribute.[29]

It is to be noted that the Code does not determine the amount of the cathedraticum but leaves this to the provincial council or to a meeting of the bishops of the province,[30] unless this amount has been determined by a custom of long standing.[31] In determining the amount, however, the words *moderata taxa* as well as *signum subiectionis* should not be lost from sight. While the cathedratic tax is not an obligation payable during the vacancy of the see,[32] it becomes due to the bishop from the very day he takes possession.[33] During the vacancy it is not due to the vicar capitular or to the diocesan administrator.[34]

The cathedraticum is due from all churches subject to the episcopal jurisdiction. This includes every parish and collegiate church, all public secular oratories and also all churches tended by religious.[35] Likewise it is due from all parish priests and canons (if any) who enjoy an individual prebend. It is evident from a letter of the Apostolic Delegate to the bishops of the United States of America, November 10, 1922, that all parishes in the United States having a resident pastor, an endowment or other sufficient resources, and defined boundaries, are benefices; and the

[29] S.C.C., *Diocesis N. et Aliarum in Gallia,* 13 mart. 1920—*AAS,* XII, (1920), 444. Cf. Bouscaren, *Canon Law Digest,* I, 720.

[30] Cf. can. 1507.

[31] Cf. can. 1509, 8°.

[32] S.C.C., resol., 20 aug. 1917—*AAS,* IX, (1917), 497. Cf. Bouscaren, *op. cit.,* I, p. 719.

[33] Can. 349, § 2.

[34] S.C.C., resol. 20 aug. 1917—*AAS,* IX, (1917), 497. Cf. Bouscaren, *loc. cit.*

[35] *AAS,* IX, (1917), 500.

pastors have all the obligations of canonical pastors.[36] Under similar circumstances and conditions all parishes in Australia, for equal reason, should be considered as benefices and thus be subject to the payment of the cathedraticum. Finally, it is also due from those confraternities[37] which have their own church, but not if they possess only a chapel or an altar in the church.

In Book V of the Code under Title XIX, which deals with the abuse of ecclesiastical authority or office, canon 2408 lists a *ferendae sententiae* penalty for those who unlawfully exact taxes or tribute. Persons who increase the amount of or exact more than the customary taxes, as legitimately approved in accordance with canon 1507, shall be restrained by means of a heavy monetary fine, and, if they fail again, they are to be suspended or removed from office, in proportion to the gravity of their guilt, without prejudice to the obligation of making restitution of the money unjustly acquired.[38]

Article 3. Extraordinary Diocesan Taxation

Having stated the obligations of the faithful both directly and indirectly[39] to support the Church and its ministers, the Code in canon 1505 expresses certain limitations as attaching to the local ordinary's power of imposing special extraordinary taxes on beneficiaries, and canon 1506 contains a prohibition against the levying of other diocesan taxes apart from the tribute levied at the time of the church's consecration and foundation.

> Besides the seminary tax sanctioned in canons 1355 and 1356, or the pension that canon 1429 allows to be imposed on a benefice, the local ordinary can in order to meet a special pressing diocesan need, impose an extraordinary and moderate

[36] Cf. Doheny, *Church Property: Modes of Acquisition*, p. 57, footnote.

[37] Cans. 707, § 2, and 708.

[38] Canon 2408.

[39] Canons 1496, 1502-1504.

> tax on all incumbents of benefices, be they religious or secular.[40]

Thus the present law preserves the tenor of the old law in restricting to a certain extent the ordinary's power of imposing taxes, as a safeguard against all undue burdening of the faithful in consequence of any misguided and indiscreet zeal.[41]

In canon 1505 the persons listed as subject to this extraordinary yet moderate tax are the incumbents of benefices. Hence benefices as such, or parishes and ecclesiastical institues as mentioned in the preceding and subsequent canon, are not subject to it. It does not matter whether the beneficiary is a secular or a religious. Exempt religious, however, are not bound by this obligation.[42] While the amount of the subsidy is not specifically determined in the law, it should be *moderate* and interpreted in accordance with the nature of the extraordinary necessity and the financial condition of the beneficiaries.

The support of the seminary is a work of such importance as to qualify it for exemption from the provisions of this canon.

> For the establishment of a seminary and the support of its students, if it lacks its own income, the bishop can:
> 1°. direct pastors or other rectors even of exempt churches to take up a collection for this purpose in church at given times;
> 2°. levy a contribution or tax in his diocese;
> 3°. if these means prove inadequate, annex some simple benefices to the seminary.[43]
>
> 1. Subject to the tax levied for the seminary are the following, without the benefit of appeal, despite any contrary custom, which is hereby rejected as unreasonable, and notwithstanding any

[40] Canon 1505.

[41] C. 6, *de censibus, exactionibus et procurationibus*, III, 39. C. 2, *de censibus, exactionibus et procurationibus*, III, 20, in VI°

[42] S.C.C., 18 febr. 1713—*Thesaurus*, IX, 224. Cf. F. Schmalzgrueber, *Ius Ecclesiasticum Universum* (5 vols. in 12, Romae 1843-1845), Lib. III, tit. 39, n. 65.

[43] Canon 1355.

contrary privilege, which is hereby abrogated: the funds serving for the bishop's table, all benefices, even those of regulars and such as are constituted under the right of patronage, all parishes and quasi-parishes, even though they should have no other income besides the offerings of the faithful, the guest house established by ecclesiastical authority, sodalities canonically established and the building funds of churches, if they have income of their own, every religious house, even if exempt, unless its support comes entirely from alms or in it there is actually conducted for the promotion of the interests of the Church a college of students or teachers.

2. This tax must be a general one and of the same proportion for all, greater or less in accordance with the needs of the seminary, but not in excess of an annual assessment of five per cent of the taxable income, and this to be decreased as the income of the seminary grows larger.

3. The income subject to tax is that which remains in a given year after the payment of fixed charges and of current expenses; but the sum available for daily distributions is not to be computed as part of the income or, if the whole income of the benefice is so earmarked, a third part of it is not to be so computed; and the offerings of the faithful are not to be counted as income or, if the entire income of a parish consists of such offerings, a third part of them is not to be so counted.[44]

Likewise does canon 1505 exempt the beneficial pension, that is the pension provided for a retired incumbent of a benefice, as expressed in canon 1429.

1. Local ordinaries cannot impose on any kind of benefices perpetual pensions or temporary pensions created for the life of the person receiving the pension, but they are authorized, for a justifying reason, to be expressed in the act of appointment, to impose on them, at the time of the appointment of an incumbent, temporary pensions created for the life of the incumbent, provided that an adequate sum is reserved to the latter.

[44] Canon 1356, §§ 1-3.

> 2. But, except for the benefit of the retiring pastor or vicar of a parish, they cannot impose pensions on parochial benefices and in any event the pensions shall not be in excess of a third of the parish income that remains after a deduction has been made for all expenses and for the income that accrued unpredictably.
>
> 3. Pensions imposed on benefices by the Roman Pontiff or by others who made appointments come to an end with the death of the pensioner, and the latter is not allowed to convey his right to others, unless that right was expressly granted him.[45]

The only other times when an ordinary is allowed to impose a tribute or a tax on churches, benefices and other ecclesiastical institutes, is the time of their juridical foundation or liturgical consecration. Only at the time of foundation or consecration can the ordinary impose any other tax for the good of the diocese or for the patron on churches, benefices, and other ecclesiastical institutes, even though they are subject to him; but in no case can a tax be imposed on manual or founded Mass stipends.[46]

This ruling is in accord with the old law that forbade the imposing of new taxes or the increasing of the previous ones.[47] In the middle ages the imposition of taxes had become so frequent and inequitable that the III General Council of the Lateran (1179) introduced stringent restrictive measures for the abrogation of such abuses.

> Prohibemus insuper, ne ad abbatibus, vel episcopis vel aliis prelatis novi census imponantur ecclesiis, nec veteres augeantur, nec partem redituum suis usibus appropriare praesumant; sed libertatem, quam sibi maiores conservare desiderant, minoribus quoque suis bona voluntate conservent. Si quis vero aliter fecerit, irritum quod egerit habeatur.[48]

[45] Canon 1429, §§ 1-3. [46] Canon 1506.

[47] Cf. Schmalzgrueber, *Ius Ecclesiasticum Universum,* Lib. III, tit. 29, n. 10.

[48] C. 7, X, *de censibus, exactionibus et procurationibus,* III, 39. See canon 7 of the Council.

In the two succeeding centuries, despite the III Lateran Council's severe prohibition, Clement III (1191)[49] and Clement V (1313)[50] were constrained to repeat similar legislation.

The Council of Trent ,while mentioning nothing about the cathedraticum or special diocesan taxes, forbade bishops to exact any fee while making their diocesan visitation.[51] The present law, adhering to the traditional legislation, makes exception only for the two occasions as mentioned in canon 1506.

Article 4. The Determination of Fees

The determination of fees in a province is left to the provincial council or to a meeting of the bishops of the province.

> 1. Without prejudice to canon 1056 and canon 1234, it belongs to a provincial council or a meeting of the bishops of a province to specify the fees payable in the entire ecclesiastical province for the various acts of voluntary jurisdiction, for the execution of rescripts of the Apostolic See, and on the occasion of the ministration of the sacraments or the sacramentals; such determination, however, has no force unless it is previously approved by the Apostolic See.
> 2. The fees for judicial acts are to be determined according to the provision of canon 1909.[52]

From the very beginning it has been the Church's desire to remove all trace and even suspicion of simony.[53] Lest payment should be associated with the reception of the sacraments, or lest offerings made on such occasions be considered as the price for them, great prudence and care have had to be exercised in their administration. Gratitude and the generosity of the faithful have engendered the custom of making an offering whenever the clergy attended

[49] C. 15, 2, *de censibus, exactionibus et procurationibus,* III, 39.
[50] C. un., *de excessibus praelatorum,* V, 6, in Clem.
[51] Sess. XXIV, *de ref.,* c. 3.
[52] Canon 1507, §§ 1-2.
[53] Cf. Acts, VIII; 18, 19.

their spiritual needs. While the offering was rather a contribution to their support or even a recompense for the extraordinary labor involved, custom brought it about that, *de facto,* offerings were made on such occasions. These were the stole fees as the faithful know them at the present time.

In the IV General Council of the Lateran (1215) Innocent III[54] declared that the sacraments were to be administered freely, but that the faithful were to conform to the praiseworthy and long-established custom of making an offering on that occasion, and that the bishops should, when it was necessary, compel them to do so. Once such a concession was granted in law limits had to be defined and the inevitable abuses corrected. Pope Innocent XI (1676-1689) formulated chancery fees and rates regulating the charges for various acts, instruments and writings sent out from chanceries in 1678.[55] Earlier the Council of Trent had forbidden the exaction of fees and the acceptance of offerings in connection with the conferring of Holy Orders.[56] On June 10, 1896, the Sacred Congregation of the Council issued a decree in which it delineated the principles in accordance with which it directed the bishops in determining the fees to be exacted or accepted in their diocese.[57]

The imposition of fees in accordance with the rules of prudence and justice in sacramental matters was permitted, provided that the sacraments were conferred freely, that pious customs were observed, and that all taint of simony was carefully obviated. In those matters that did not involve the administration of the sacraments, as for example, the granting of dispensations, laudable customs were to be observed and prudent consideration given to temporal, local, and personal factors. The poor were to be exempt from all

[54] C. 42. X, *de simonia et ne aliquid pro spiritualibus exigatur vel promittatur,* V, 3. See canon 66 of the Council.

[55] *Bullarium Innocentii* XI, VIII, 61. Ferraris, *Prompta Bibliotheca,* s.v. *Taxa,* n. 1.

[56] Sess. XXI, *de ref.,* c. 1.

[57] Cf. *Fontes,* n. 4298.

taxes, and for all persons the fees were not to be so great as to deter any of them from the reception of the sacraments. If there was any danger of concubinage, matrimonial fees were to waived.[58]

In a resolution of December 11, 1920,[59] the Sacred Congregation of the Council specifically criticized the schedule which as sent for approval by a certain province specified a range of fees within which the respective bishops of the province were free to make a choice. In the same case the Sacred Congregation insisted that no charge can be made except for the actual material used, i.e., not for the writing or the trouble involved in the granting of the following faculties: for the exercise of the power of orders; for the administration of the sacraments; for preaching; for the transfer and interment of the remains of the deceased. It disapproved of a heavier fee for the same service when charged against priests who came from outside the diocese. It ordered expunged all mention of any fee to be paid the bishop on the occasion of his conferring benefices.[60] This resolution referred to the decree of the Sacred Congregation of the Council of June 10, 1896, and to the letter of Innocent XI, *Essendo avuto,* of October 8, 1678.[61]

In canon 1507, § 1, particular attention is drawn to the ruling of canons 1506 and 1234. Canon 1506 permits a modest fee, from those who can afford it, to defray office expenses in the granting of dispensations. The Sacred Congregation of the Council would approve no other charge or fees.[62] Fees for dispensations obtained directly from the Holy See may include the following items: *expensae,* i.e., the cost of mailing, translation, stationery, etc.; *agentia,* the commission of an agent at Rome; *taxa;* the definite and fixed fee, always the same for the same impediment;

[58] *AAS,* XXIX, (1896), 433-435; Cf. *Fontes,* n. 4298.

[59] *AAS,* XIII, (1921), 350; Bouscaren, *Canon Law Digest,* I, 720.

[60] Cf. Abbo-Hannan, *The Sacred Canons,* II, 715.

[61] S.C.C., resol., 11 dec. 1920—*AAS,* XIII, (1921), 350; Bouscaren, *op. cit.,* I, 720.

[62] *AAS,* XIII, (1921),, 350; Bouscaren, *op. cit.,* I, 504.

componenda, i.e., an alms determined by the financial status of the petitioner and the nature of the impediment (in contemplation of a proportionate reparation made for the failure to obey the law). In sending petitions to the Holy See the local ordinary is to note the financial status of the petitioner.[63] Canon 1234 permits local ordinaries, after consultation with the diocesan consultors, to draw up a list of funeral fees or offerings. Within that schedule and to remove every occasion of quarreling or of scandal, they are to define with moderation the rights of all concerned in the various cases that may occur.[64]

Canon 1507, § 1, has an important bearing on the other canons in the Code that deal with the pastor's right to offerings and stole fees. Canon 463 states the pastor's right to offerings and stole fees which approved custom or lawful taxation has authorized in accordance with the norm of canon 1507, § 1. Likewise canon 736, with reference to the administration of the sacraments, strictly limits the reception of offerings to whatever is duly sanctioned. To further the observance of this canon there are several relevant decrees of the IV Plenary Council that clarify a pastor's position and obviate difficulties and discord between neighboring pastors.

> "All offerings which are given on the occasion of a baptism, of a marriage, or at a funeral belong to the pastor within whose parish these ministrations are performed, unless there be evidence of a divergent intention on the part of the donors with reference to the sum that exceeds the normal fee, with due allowance also made for the ruling contained in decree no. 476.[65]

This latter decree recommends that, if a marriage is celebrated in another place with the permission of the proper pastor, half the marriage fee be returned to the pastor of the bride.[66]

[63] Abbo-Hannan, *op. cit.,* II, 231.
[64] Cf. canon 1234.
[65] *Concil. Plen. Aust. IV,* dec. n. 668.
[66] Cf. *ibid.,* decree no. 476.

Furthermore, if a pastor unlawfully administers the sacraments or sacramentals (as mentioned in the preceding decree) to the faithful who are not his subjects, he is bound in justice as soon as possible to remit the offering to the rightful pastor.[67] The council applies the same rule even to those priests who by reason of friendship or relationship perform such functions.[68]

The above listed decrees treat of those offerings or fees which are given on the occasion of the administration of the sacraments or of the exercise of pastoral duties. Nevertheless, to remove any doubt that may arise concerning the ownership of offerings, gifts or donations given on other occasions, decree no. 666 states the presumption to be in favor of the church.

> Unless the contrary is established the things that are given to pastors or rectors of churches, even if such churches are entrusted to religious, are presumed to be gifts left to the church.[69]

Canon 1507, § 1, therefore, is broad in scope. Seen in its relation to the above-mentioned canons and decrees, it is an important norm for the regulating of points of law and discipline which are of frequent occurrence. The interest of the Church and its ministers will be safeguarded, and difficulties and discord will thereby be happily removed.

The second section of canon 1507 concerns fees and taxes for judicial acts. These are adequately provided for in canon 1909, as is therein stated, and they pertain to that section of the Code.

Article 5. Prescription

Canon 1508 states that, with due regard to the canons that follow, the Church, in relation to ecclesiastical property, adopts prescription as it stands in the legislation of the respective nations, as a means of acquiring property and of freeing oneself of obligations.[70] Thus canon 1508 declares that the Church recognizes the enactments of civil

[67] *Ibid.*, decree no. 669.
[68] Cf. *ibid.*, decree 670
[69] *Ibid.*, decree n. 666.
[70] Canon 1508.

law in matters of prescription, provided that these latter do not violate the rulings of canons 1509-1512.

Apart from a lengthy survey of the historical-juridical concept of prescription from Roman Law, whence it took its origin, through its development in the early and medieval Church, it will suffice to say in this connection that the Church, in conformity with all its previous legislation, continues to recognize prescription as a just means of acquiring rights or freeing oneself from obligations, provided that the rulings of canon law are observed. Before the advent of the present Code the general basis for the rules of ecclesiastical prescription was Roman Law, modified to conform to the spirit of the Church.[71] The present law, however, as stated in canon 1508, accepts certain portions of civil law and incorporates them as part of its own law.

In canon law, prescription is generally understood as a legally approved method, by which through a continued possession or use, according to the accepted method or requisite lapse of time, there is obtained some right to property (*usucapio*) or some freedom from obligations (*praescriptio*). Considered as a mere *exceptio* it may be defined as a peremptory exception through which a possessor in good faith after a lapse of a specified time can repel a former owner from establishing his right.[72]

In English Law, prescription, as a means of acquiring title, is composed of three different institutes; *adverse possession, prescription,* and the *limitation of actions.* It is based on the statute of 1623 passed in the reign of James I entitled *"An Act for Limitation of Actions, and for Avoiding Suits of Law"*[73] In *adverse possession* and *prescription* the lapse of a prescribed period of time as well as the actual adverse possession is required, while the third method, the *limitation of actions,* merely deprives a negligent creditor of his right to enforce his claim in court because of his

[71] C. 1, X. *de novi operis nunciatione,* V, 32.

[72] Wernz-Vidal, *Ius Canonicum,* Vol. IV, *De Rebus,* Pars. II, n. 818, p. 301.

[73] 21 James 1, c. 16.

failure to enforce it within a prescribed time. *Adverse possession* refers to corporeal property, e.g., land or goods in general; *prescription* refers to incorporeal property, e.g., a right of way across another's land. This latter kind of title rests on a presumed grant, while the title to corporeal property by adverse possession is based on the circumstances of possession. The period of time required for the obtaining of title to land by adverse possession is always longer than that which is required for the obtaining of title to movable property.[74]

In the State of New South Wales the period of time is generally regarded as twenty years, though there are no statutes to that effect. The title to incorporeal rights depends upon grants. In England a title to such a right might also be derived from immemorial user, the time of legal memory being fixed at the beginning of the reign of Richard I. Proof of user as of right, for twenty years or upwards, was considered to afford a presumption of immemorial enjoyment.[75] This presumption could, however, be effectively rebutted by proof that the enjoyment had in fact commenced within the time of legal memory.[76] This law, however, did not take effect in New South Wales, where there is not any such thing as immemorial usage.[77] There can, therefore, be no title by prescription on this ground.[78]

The *Prescription Act of England*[79] is not in force in New South Wales, and there is no local statute giving such a mode of title.[80] It seems, however, that the fiction of a lost grant may be resorted to, and that under some circumstances the existence of such an instrument may be presumed, as, e.g., when there has been uninterrupted user of

[74] Abbo-Hannan, *The Sacred Canons*, II, 716.

[75] Rex v. Joffiffe, 2 B. & C., 54; 2 Wms. Saund. 175a et seq.

[76] Cf. Jenkins v. Harvey, 1 Cr. M. & R. 894.

[77] *Vickery v. Marr*, 4 S.C.R., Eq. 66, 69.

[78] Stephens v. McClung, 4 S.C.R., Eq. 71.

[79] 2 & 3 Wm. IV. c. 71.

[80] Vickery v. Marr, 5 S.C.R., 202, 206.

a road for upwards of twenty years,[81] but no such presumption can be made against the crown in respect of a right of way.[82]

Other conditions of the possession postulated for giving title, both for adverse possession and prescription, are that the possession be definite, hostile to the claim of those out of possession, widely known, enjoyed under a claim of right and in good faith, continuous, uninterrupted and peaceable. Good faith is presumed in the absence of proof to the contrary. All the above listed elements are similar to the conditions required by canon law before prescription can be invoked. These are five in number, and their existence must be proved, and not simply presumed.[83]

First, the object must be prescriptible. Some things by their very nature, or because of the prohibition of canon law, or in consequence of the incapacity of the person seeking to claim prescription, cannot be subject to prescription.[84]

Secondly, good faith is required, not only in the beginning but also throughout the whole period of possession, as it was required by the IV General Council of the Lateran (1215),[85] and is now required by canon 1512.

Thirdly, while there is no express mention of title in the Code this necessarily is implied, for possession must begin with some kind of title, as was required in the law of decretals.[86] Canon 1446 legalizes an exceptional form of prescription in virtue of which peaceful possession of a

[81] 4 S.C.R., Eq. 74. Municipality of Waterloo v. Hinchcliffe, 5 S.C.R., 273.

[82] Richard E. Kemp, *Principles of the Law of Real Property* (Sydney: The Law Book Co., of Australiasia Ltd., 1903), Part IV of Title, p. 513 f.

[83] Cf. Wernz-Vidal, *Ius Canonicum,* IV *De Rebus,* Pars II, no. 821-28, pp. 305-313.

[84] Cf. canon 1509.

[85] C. 20, X, *de praescriptionibus,* II, 26. Reg. 2, 3, R.J., in VI°. "Possessor malae fidei ullo tempore non praescribit": "Sine Possessione praescriptio non procedit."

[86] C. 17, X, *de praescriptionibus,* 11, 26.

benefice in good faith for thee years with a title, even though invalid, suffices for the securing of the benefice by lawful prescription. "If a cleric who possesses a benefice shall prove that he was in good faith in the peaceful possession of that benefice for an entire period of three years, even though with an invalid title, provided of course that no simony was involved, he obtains the benefice through legitimate prescription."[87]

Fourthly, in accordance with the maxim in the *Regula Juris*: "Sine possessione praescriptio non procedit,"[88] a just possession is necessary. This must be in one's own name, continuous and not interrupted, peaceable and safe, excluding all forcible precarious possessions.[89]

Fifthly, the time postulated by the law must have elapsed. In this matter canon 1511 specifies the time for some objects. Other objects are left to the enactments of the civil laws of the respective countries in accordance with canon 1508. Hence there could be considerable variation in different places.

Canon 1509 enumerates things that are not amenable to prescription. Four refer to liberative prescription, namely, nos. 1, 5, 7, and 8; and four to acquisitive prescription, nos. 2, 3, 4 and 6. The following are not subject to prescription:

1. A right that is accorded by the natural or the positive divine law.[90] Hence an object obtained by theft, in violation of the natural divine law, obtained through usurpation, in violation of positive divine law, could never be secured by prescription.

2. That which can be obtained only by Apostolic privilege.[91]

3. Spiritual rights for which the laity has no capacity, when such prescription would eventuate as a favor for

[87] Canon 1446.
[88] Reg. 3, R.J., in VI°
[89] Wernz-Vidal, *ibid.*, n. 824, p. 307.
[90] Canon 1509, 1°.
[91] Canon 1509, 2°.

the laity.[92] Thus a lay person cannot by prescription obtain any rights to ecclesiastical jurisdiction, benefices or ecclesiastical pensions.[93]

4. Definite and undisputed boundaries of ecclesiastical provinces, dioceses, parishes, apostolic vicariates, apostolic prefectures, abbacies *nullius* and prelacies *nullius*.[94]

5. Stipends and the attached obligations for the application of Masses.[95] A mutual understanding is established between the donor of the Mass stipends and the priest obliged to say the Masses. Nevertheless, while liberation from the obligation of their application is thus forbidden, the transfer of this obligation from one to another is not.[96]

6. An ecclesiastical benefice in the absence of title.[97] According to canon 147, § 1, an ecclesiastical office cannot validly be obtained apart from a canonical filling of the office. At the very least some semblance of a title (*titulus coloratus*) is always required.

7. The right of visitation and the rightful claim for obedience, with the effect that those subject thereto would be liberated from visitation by any prelate and from the obligation of obedience to any prelates.[98]

8. The payment of the Cathedratic tax.[99]

Canon 1510 treats of legal prescription with reference to sacred things.[100] Sacred things owned by private persons can be acquired by private persons through prescription, but the latter cannot devote them to uses that are not sacred; but if they have lost their consecration or blessing, they can be acquired even for such use without restriction,

[92] Canon 1509, 3°.
[93] Cf. canon 118.
[94] Canon 1509, 4°.
[95] Canon 1509, 5°.
[96] Cf. Wernz, *Ius Decretalium*, III, n. 300.
[97] Canon 1509, 6°.
[98] Canon 1509, 7°.
[99] Canon 1509, 8°. Cf. commentary on canon 1504, *supra*, p. 47.
[100] Cf. canon 1497, § 2.

but not for sordid use.[101] While sacred things belonging to one person may be acquired through legal prescription by another, they may not be diverted to profane use. This is in accord with the axiom, "semel Deo dicatum non est ad usus humanos ulterius transferendum."[102] Canon 1150 furthermore enjoins that consecrated and blessed objects should be reverently treated and not put to profane use even if they are in the possession of individuals. If, however, they have already lost their blessing or consecration,[103] they may be freely acquired for profane, but not for unbecoming, uses. Sacred things when owned not by private persons cannot be acquired through legal prescription by a private person. They can, however, be acquired through legal prescription by one ecclesiastical moral person against another.[104] There is no legal restriction that prevents an ecclesiastical moral person from acquiring through legal prescription sacred things from an individual.[105]

The interval required for prescription against ecclesiastical moral persons and the good faith that is necessary are stated in canons 1511 and 1512.

1. A period of one hundred years is required for the operation of prescription against the immovable property of the Apostolic See, and also against precious movable property belonging to it, as well as all rights and claims at law, whether personal or real, pertaining to it.

2. A period of thirty years is required in the case of other ecclesiastical moral persons.[106]

The canon relating to the property of the Apostolic See[107] is consistent with the traditional legislation on this matter.[108] The thirty-year period for other ecclesiastical

[101] Canon 1510, § 1.
[102] Reg. 51, R.J., in VI°.
[103] Canon 1305, § 1.
[104] Canon 1510, § 2.
[105] C. 3, X, *de praescriptionibus*, II, 26.
[106] Canon 1511, §§ 1, 2.
[107] Canons 7; 100, § 1; 262.
[108] C. 16, 17, C. XVI, q. 3: c. 13, 14, 17, *de praescriptionibus*, II, 26.

moral persons is now in conformity, generally, with European civil laws.[109]

Prescription is of no avail unless it is founded on good faith not only at the beginning of possession but also during the whole period of possession requisite for the legal prescription.[110] Canon law insists on good faith throughout the whole period of the time postulated for the prescription. The virtue of justice and the individual's conscientious responsibility before God demand that such be the case. If good faith is lacking at any stage, there is a violation of justice. Since moral persons always retain the same identity, the good faith of subsequent administrators or officials could not counteract or offset the bad faith of their predecessors.

The Code's legislation on prescription, following as it does precise and traditional legal principles, harmonies ecclesiastical and civil law. By allowing the operation of the latter when compatible with justice the supreme legislator has removed the danger of the conflict so prevalent in the past, and has paved the way for a clear and peaceable understanding between Church and State.

Article 6. Donations and Bequests for Pious Causes

A. Rights of Owners to Bequeath or Devise to the Church

Provided he is not restricted by the natural or the ecclesiastical law an owner may dispose of his property, whether personal or real, to whomsoever he wishes. A restriction from the natural law, for example, requires that parents, if they have a superfluity of this world's goods, leave suitable or at least sufficient means to their children. A restriction from ecclesiastical law in canon 583 limits the right of simply professed religious in religious congregations to bequeath or devise property.[111]

[109] Cf. Doheny, *Church Property: Modes of Acquisition*, p. 79.
[110] Canon 1512.
[111] Cf. canon 583.

The present law which as enunciated in canon 1513 declares the right of individuals to donate, bequeath or devise property is but a re-statement of the Church's attitude and of the manner of acting of the faithful from Apostolic times[112] and of subsequent legislation vindicating the Church's rights as a beneficiary.[113]

> 1. He who under the natural and the ecclesiastical law may freely dispose of his goods, may leave them to pious causes either during his lifetime (*per actum inter vivos*) or in contemplation of his death (*per actum mortis causa*).
>
> 2. In last wills favoring the Church the formalities of the civil law should, if possible, be observed: if, however, these were not observed, the heirs are to be admonished to carry out the intention of the testator.[114]

A *last will* or *testament* is the expression, in the manner required by law, and operative for no purpose until death, of that which a person may lawfully require to be done after his death. *Testament,* once applied to personalty only, now is synonymous with *will.* A *codicil* is an addition to a formal will, explaining, confirming, adding to, subtracting from, or otherwise changing it. The prior will plus the codicils makes a new will. The person making a will is called a *testator*. The essential distinguishing characteristic of a will is that it has absolutely no effect as a legal instrument until the death of the testator, and is revocable until that time.

A will may be *oral* (nuncupative) or*written.* Nuncupative wills of personalty made before witnesses are good in most jurisdictions. Generally, however, only sailors and soldiers on active service and persons in contemplation of impending death can make a nuncupative will. The formally attested written will is the safest and the most usual form

[112] Cf. Acts, V: 1-4. John, XII: 6; XIII: 29.

[113] C. 4, 9, C. XIII, q. 2; cc. 2, 5, 19, X, *de testamentis et ultimis voluntatibus,* III, 26; c. un., *de testamentis et ultimis voluntatibus,* III, 6, in Clem.

[114] Canon 1513, §§ 1, 2.

of will. The document may be holographic, i.e., all in one's own handwriting, or it may be typewritten or printed. It must be signed by the testator and at least two (2) witnesses in the sight and the presence of one another—all signing at the same time.[115]

A *devise* is a testamentary disposition of realty: a *bequest* is a testamentary disposition of personalty. When the bequest is of money only, it is called a *legacy*. Hence in the drawing up of wills the usual phrases which occur are "give and devise," "give and bequeath" or "give, devise and bequeath."

A "pious will, i.e., a last will favoring the Church, includes all gifts made for a pious cause, whether *inter vivos* or *mortis causa*. The Commission for the Authentic Interpretation of the Code in reply to the query whether the word "*moneantur*" in canon 1513, § 2, was preceptive or merely exhortatory, stated that its import was such that thereby a will becomes enforceable and that it implies more than a mere caution or warning for the heirs. That is to say, by canon 1513, § 2, the fulfilment of "pious wills" becomes obligatory on the heirs even if the legal formalities which would be required to make the obligation binding in civil law are omitted.[116]

It is clear from canon 1516 that "fiduciary gifts" may be made not only by last will and testament but also by acts *inter vivos*. Property so dedicated to a "pious cause" becomes strictly ecclesiastical property and is called a "pious foundation," *only* in case it is given to some moral person in the Church.[117]

A restriction, hortatory in nature, is contained in the present legislation for the clergy of Australia and New Zealand. The Fathers of the IV Plenary Council, solicitous lest the material wealth or property of the clergy should

[115] A specimen copy of a "Form of Will" is included at the end of this work.

[116] *AAS*, XXII (1930), 196; cf. Bouscaren, *Canon Law Digest*, I, 725.

[117] Cf. canon 1497, § 1 and 1544. Cf. Bouscaren, *op. cit.*, I, 725.

become a scandal to the faithful, enacted several relevant, though exhortatory, decrees concerning the disposal thereof, either by last will or by donation *per actum inter vivos.*

> The Council strongly exhorts all priests to dispose of their goods at an opportune time lest perhaps upon death they leave a large sum of money, which is always a scandal to the faithful.[118]
>
> All priests are to make a will and those who administer ecclesiastical porperty are to leave a copy of their will in the diocesan curia.[119]
>
> All administrators of ecclesiastical goods are to choose a priest as an executor. If they choose several executors, one at least is to be a priest.[120]
>
> All priests are strongly advised that they neither give nor bequeath money which they have received from their office, even though it is not a benefice strictly so called, to strangers or relatives not in need of it.[121]
>
> The Council recommends that in disposing of their worldly goods either through donations or by last will, priests should be mindful of the diocesan seminary and of diocesan works for the fostering of vocations.[122]

The foregoing decrees are so just, so reasonable and, indeed, so praiseworthy as to need no comment.

B. FULFILMENT AND EXECUTION OF DONOR'S INTENTION

In accepting donations and last wills the Church accepts an inviolable trust and assumes a sacred obligation. Canon 1514 is, therefore, eminently practical and broad in scope. It states:

> The wishes of the faithful donating or leaving a portion of their wealth to pious causes, whether during their lifetime or in contemplation of death, must be most diligently fulfilled, even with regard to the method of administration and the distribution of the property, in line with the prescript contained in canon 1515, § 3.

[118] *Concil. Plen. Austral. IV*, decr. n. 70, p. 13.

[119] Cf. *ibid.*, n. 71.

[120] Cf. *ibid.*, n. 72.

[121] Cf. *ibid.*, n. 73.

[122] Cf. *ibid.*, n. 74.

This canon is also a restatement of the earlier legislation as found in the Decretals[123] and in the law enacted by the Council of Trent.[124] Suffice it to say that the natural law surely enjoins that the devisor's rights be respected as far as is humanly possible; and that Christian charity and justice demand the exact fulfilment of pious legacies and wills, lest the faithful be scandalized—as they surely would be—if the wishes of the dead were disregarded. So important and serious is the trust thus undertaken that canon 2348 authorizes an ordinary to coerce, even by censure, those who neglect to fufill the terms of testamentary bequests, even if these are held only in trust.[125]

In canon 1515 the ordinary is by the very disposition of the law itself (*ipso iure*) appointed an executor of all pious wills.

> 1. Ordinaries are the executors of all pious donations made in contemplation of death or during the lifetime of the donors.
>
> 2. In virtue of this right ordinaries can and must exercise vigilance even to the extent of visitation in order that the wishes of the donors may be carried out; other delegated executors must, when they have completed their task, render an account of them.
>
> 3. Clauses inserted in last wills contrary to this right of ordinaries are to be considered as not having been inserted.[126]

The present law, in so far as it uses the term *"ordinarii,"* is more extensive than the Tridentine legislation,[127] which simply empowered bishops to act as executors of all pious wills. Hence there are included, according to canon 198,

[123] C. 4, 9-11, C. XIII, q. 2: c. 4, C. XVII, q. 4: C. 3, 4, 6, 17, 19, X, *de testamentis et ultimis voluntatibus*, III, 26: c. 3, X, *de successionibus ab intestato*, III, 27.

[124] Sess. VII, *de ref.*, c. 15.

[125] Cf. canon 2348.

[126] Canon 1515, §§ 1, 2, 3.

[127] Sess. XII, *de ref.*, c. 8: "Episcopi, etiam tamquam sedis apostolicae delegati, in casibus a iure concessis omnium piarum dispositionum tam in ultima voluntate quam inter vivos sint exsecutores."

§ 1, vicars and prefects apostolic as well as major superiors of clerical exempt religious institutes. Ordinaries should take care that their duty and function in this matter be neither misunderstood nor exaggerated. The very fact that the law appoints them executors of all pious wills does not put them in the same category as an executor appointed by the testator (*testamentarius*) or by a court of law (*dativus*). Their function is to make sure, either themselves or through their delegate, that the dispositions of the will, in so far as they pertain to pious causes, are exactly fulfilled, and that the legal executors render them an account that this has been done.[128]

Decree no. 682 of the IV Plenary Council, after restating the first paragraph of canon 1515, adds the injunction that every Catholic who has goods in trust or holds bequests for pious causes should inform the ordinary as soon as possible.[129] This may be done most expeditiously through the pastor of the parish, who is usually the first to be made aware of such bequests, and on whom therefore indirectly devolves the obligation of informing the ordinary.

Decrees nos. 683, 684, and 685 are but the restatement of canon 1516, §§21, 2, 3.

> 1. A cleric or a religious, if he has been entrusted by the donor during his lifetime or in a will with property to be devoted to pious causes, must inform the ordinary of his trust, and must report to him all the items of movable or immovable property involved together with the burdens imposed; and if the donor should expressly and absolutely forbid this, the commission shall not be accepted.
>
> 2. The ordinary must demand that property thus entrusted shall be safely invested and must likewise exercise vigilance over the fulfilment of the pious wish according to the norm of canon 1515.
>
> 3. For property given to any religious in trust, if it is given to the churches of the place or of the diocese, for the benefit of the people, or in further-

[128] Cf. Beste, *Introductio in Codicem,* p. 753.

[129] Cf. *Concil. Plen. Austral. IV.,* decr. n. 682.

> ance of pious causes, the ordinary mentioned in §§ 1, 2, is the local ordinary; otherwise the ordinary thus mentioned is the proper ordinary of the religious himself.

Whenever gifts are made, whether during the lifetime of the donor or at his death, a cleric or religious must inform the ordinary. Though a lay person may not be obliged, in virtue of this canon, to make a report, he is obliged by the ruling of degree no. 682 to do so.[130] In addition he is bound to submit to the inspection of the local ordinary and to render an account of his administration in virtue of canon 1515, § 2. What constitutes a safe investment would depend upon the nature and condition of the country's economy at the time the investment is to be made. In general, government bonds, *"gilt edged"* securities and real estate may be considered safe investments.

To keep pace in an ever-changing world with social, financial and economic changes, conditions and dispositions of wills are often difficult to fulfill. A will made in one generation and unchanged at the testator's death may have to be relaxed, respecified or modified if it is to meet the conditions of the present time. Such mutations, unless other provisions are made in the will itself, may only be carried out by the Apostolic See.

> 1. The relaxation, specification or modication of last wills, which should be made only for a just and necessary reason, is reserved to the Apostolic See, unless the founder expressly granted authority also to the local ordinary.
>
> 2. But if, because of diminished income or for some other reason, through no fault of the administrator, the fulfilment of the imposed obligations has become impossible, then also the ordinary, after hearing the interested parties, and carrying out the intention of the founder in a manner as exact as possible, may authorize an equitable retrenchment of the obligations, except such as attach to Masses, the relaxation of which is always exclusively reserved to the Apostolic See.[131]

[130] Cf. *supra*, p. 71 and canon 13, § 2.

[131] Canon 1517, §§ 1, 2.

The listed legislation along with the other canons of this section is the result of centuries of experience. It perpetuates the earlier law[132] as also that of the Council of Trent.[133] Relxation points to a reduction in the number of the acts; specification relates to the proportions of the plan; modification substitutes acts, plans or beneficiaries for the ones it supplants.[134]

A just and necessary reason would be present when a more advantageous use of the gift is possible. It is to be noted, however, that only the Holy See, and not the ordinary, has the right to decide what is a justifying necessity. On the other hand, the local ordinary can relax, specify or modify a will only when it is impossible to carry out the donor's wishes. Legal impossibility as arising from prohibitions of canon law or civil law as well as moral impossibility would furnish a sufficient reason.[135]

In Australia, pursuant to English Law, the application of the *"cy pres"* doctrine is possible. The meaning of this doctrine is that, when a specified duty or function is to be performed but it cannot be done in exact conformity with the scheme of the testator, it must be performed with as close an approximation to that scheme as is reasonably practicable. It follows from this principle that when there is both a general and a particular intent, but the particular one is rendered ineffectual, then the phraseology is to be so construed as to give effect to the general intent of the donor. So, compared with canon 1517, § 2, it is very similar.[136]

[132] C. 14, C. XVI, q. 1.

[133] Sess. VII, *de ref.*, c. 15; sess. XXII, *de ref.*, c. 6.

[134] Cf. De Meester, *Compendium*, II, n. 1470.

[135] Cf. J. Hannan, *The Canon Law of Wills* (Philadelphia; The Dolphin Press, 1934), n. 797.

[136] Doheny, *Church Property: Modes of Acquisition*, p. 98.

CHAPTER IV

THE ADMINISTRATION OF ECCLESIASTICAL GOODS

ARTICLE 1. THE NOTION OF ADMINISTRATION. THE ROMAN PONTIFF, THE SUPREME ADMINISTRATOR

A. THE NOTION OF ADMINISTRATION

Upon a duly vindicated claim of the Church's right of ownership, which has been treated in the preceding chapters, there logically follows in the Code its legislation concerning the rights and duties of those within whose authority it is, from the Supreme Pontiff down through local ordinaries and pastors, to conserve, to make productive and to derive use and benefit from the temporal possessions of the Church. With the Church's divine right to acquire and hold temporal goods duly established, it follows that the Church has a similar right and duty to conserve and use them in furtherance of the salvation of souls. The canons of the Code and the decrees of the IV Plenary Council here treated do not deal with property belonging to religious institutes. This consideration receives treatment exclusively in canons 531—537, but it does not bear any direct relevance to the topic here to be explored.

The administration of church goods, in so far as it differs from their acquisition and alienation, includes the control and care of the temporal goods of the Church with a view to having them fully serve the purpose for which they were acquired. Hence, administration includes all those acts that are necessary or useful to keep the property in good repair and condition, to make it productive, to derive profit from it and, in general, to apply, disburse and use its return for charitable and legitimate purposes.[1]

[1] Cf. Beste, *Introductio in Codicem,* p. 756. James McManus, *The Administration of Temporal Goods in Religious Institutes,* The Catholic University of America Canon Law Studies, n. 109 (Washington, D.C.: The Catholic University of America, 1937), p. 12.

Acts of administration may be either *ordinary,* such as the acts which are necessary for the usual management of affairs and which do not require the permission of or reference to a higher authority, e.g., the payment of weekly or monthly accounts, the making of minor repairs, etc., or they may be *extraordinary,* such as the acts of greater importance and of less frequent occurrence which require the permission of higher authority, e.g., the buying or selling of land, the making of extensive repairs or renovations, the erection of new buildings, etc. Acts of ordinary administration are those which the administrator may perform validly by reason of his office and without the permission of the local ordinary. It may happen sometimes, if some of these acts which are necessary as part of the administrative office are of greater moment, that the law may require the ordinary's permission for the lawful performance of the acts. Nonetheless they are valid if performed without his permission as long as they still pertain to ordinary administration. If, however, the law states that an act is invalid apart from the required permission, or if it requires a special faculty in the administrator before his act will be considered valid, then the acts of administration that are so conditioned are to be considered acts of extraordinary administration.[2]

The IV Plenary Council specifies and earmarks as extraordinary such acts of administration which involve the *selling, exchange, or removal* of ecclesiastical goods in notable amount.

> In accordance with the norms of canons 1530, 1531, 1532, with reference namely to the selling, exchange or removal of ecclesiastical goods, all administrators of such cannot act except in matters of lesser importance, unless they have obtained permission for this beforehand from the lawful authority. The act will be invalid if this authority was not obtained.[3]

[2] McManus, *op. cit.,* p. 82. Cf. canons 1530, 1531, 1532, and Decr. n°. 664.

[3] *Concil. Plen. Austral. IV,* Decr. n. 664.

What constitutes matters of lesser importance is not specified by the Council. This specification seems left to the particular diocesan statutes, which should be so framed as to take account of the specific indults granted through the Sacred Congregation for the Propagation of the Faith for the administration and alienation of Church property.

B. THE ROMAN PONTIFF, THE SUPREME ADMINISTRATOR OF ECCLESIASTICAL PROPERTY

The Roman Pontiff is the supreme administrator and dispenser of all ecclesiastical property.[4] The power of the Roman Pontiff is designated as supreme. That is to say, he has the right to administer both immediately and mediately any ecclesiastical property whatever. Immediate administration means the direct management of ecclesiastical property. Mediate administration signifies the indirect management of property through legislation.[5] This right of supreme administration and dispenation belongs to the pope, not as to an owner or possessor of the ecclesiastical goods, but as to the principal guardian of them in that he is constituted as the very head of the Church. It is his prerogative to establish the general norms to be observed by all moral personalities in the Church in the acquisition and administration of their goods.[6]

As supreme adiminstrator of all ecclesiastical property the pope may exercise all administrative acts without any subjection to rules conditioned by the ordinary or extraordinary nature of the acts requisite for the control and the care of the property. This right is based upon his supreme and immediate jurisdiction over the Universal Church and all units within it.[7] In point of fact, as the following

[4] Canon 1518.

[5] Joseph J. Comyns, *Papal and Episcopal Administration of Church Property*, The Catholic University of America Canon Law Studies, n. 147 (Washington, D.C.: The Catholic University of America Press, 1942), p. 57.

[6] Cf. canons 218, § 1 and 1499, § 2.

[7] Cf. canon 218, §§ 1, 2. Matthaeus Conte a Coronata, *Institutiones*

canons show and in line with the norms therein stated, the actual administration is left to those who hold an ordinary jurisdiction, such as local ordinaries and pastors, or who enjoy some specific administrative capacity, under the jurisdiction of the Apostolic See.

ARTICLE 2. THE ADMINISTRATION OF CHURCH PROPERTY

A. THE DUTY OF THE LOCAL ORDINARY HIMSELF

> It is the duty of the local ordinary in his territory carefuly to watch over the administration of all ecclesiastical property which has not been withdrawn from his jurisdiction, with due regard for the more extensive rights which he may enjoy through legitimate prescriptions.[8]

This duty of supervision which the ordinary must exercise includes, during the time of his episcopal visitation,[9] the right not only of demanding an account of all the administrative acts, but also of inspecting the books, of receiving an auditor's report, etc. As the local ordinary supervises the administration of only the diocesan property, he may not interfere in the administration of property belonging to exempt religious in his diocese. In his office of supervisor, however, he can compel clerics to comply with the requirements of the civil law for the purpose of safeguarding the ecclesiastical property.[10]

The second paragraph of canon 1519 is in reality an exhortation to ordinaries to specify, through their own diocesan statutes, the limits of power for administrators in accordance with whatever faculties the Holy See has extended to the diocese, and to leave the actual administration to their appointees for them faithfully to carry out by obeying the spirit and the letter of the law. The ordinary's function, therefore, is rather one of vigilance and super-

Iuris Canonici (5 vols., Taurini; Marietti, 1928-1936), II, *De Rebus*, p. 471 (hereafter cited as *Institutiones*).

[8] Canon 1519, § 1.

[9] Cf. canons 343-346.

[10] S.C. de Prop. Fide, 27 maii 1881—*Coll. S.C.P.F.*, no. 1553.

vision than, with the exception of the *mensa episcopalis*, one of immediate administration of the various diocesan units.

> With due regard for vested rights, lawful customs and the circumstances involved, ordinaries shall take care to regulate the whole business of the administration of ecclesiastical property through special opportune instructions given within the limits of the general law.[11]
>
> For the proper discharge of this duty every ordinary shall establish in his episcopal city a council, which shall consist of a president, who shall be the ordinary himself, and of two or more qualified men who are, if possible, experts also in civil law, and who are chosen by the ordinary after conultation with the chapter (diocesan consultors), unless by law or particular custom provision has legitimately been made in some other equivalent fashion.[12]

The particular law for Australasia is stated in decree no 654.

> In each diocese there is to be established a council of vigilance for the administration of ecclesiastical goods, the members of which council are to take the oath faithfully to fulfill their offce.[13]

It is from the members of this council that the trustees for the supervision and the administration of Roman Catholic Church Trust Property are drawn.[14]

> To prevent ecclesiastical property from falling into the hands of others the bishop will take care that title deeds and instruments be drawn up in the name of at least three guardians nominated by the ordinary of the place. Among these will be the bishop of the diocese and at least two priests prudent and skilled in matters of this kind. These must meet once a year to watch over the security of the property. If any one of these had been

[11] Canon 1519, § 2.

[12] Canon 1520, § 1.

[13] *Concil. Plen. Austral. IV*, decr. no. 654.

[14] Cf. *supra*, Chapter II, p. 35.

> removed for any cause the bishop must appoint another in his place.[15]
>
> In the absence of an apostolic indult, there are not to be appointed to the post of administrator those who are related to the ordinary in the first or second degree of consanguinity or affinity.
>
> When important administrative acts are to be performed, the local ordinary shall not fail to consult the council of administration; the members of it have, however, only an advisory capacity, unless their consent is required either in cases especially recounted in the general law or in consequence of the articles of foundation.
>
> The members of this council shall, in the presence of the ordinary, take an oath that they will efficiently and faithfully fulfill their office.[16]

If the ordinary were to act without consulting his administrative council, it seems that his action would be merely unlawful.[17] Only when the council's advice or consent is required in the cases named or listed in the law, or in virtue of special articles in the charter of foundation, would his neglect of their advice and consent result in an invalid act.[18]

B. THE APPOINTMENT OF ADMINISTRATORS BY THE LOCAL ORDINARY

To embrace the broader aspects of the local ordinary's power of supervision and administration the Code states that, in addition to the establishment of a diocesan council of administration, the local ordinary shall appoint administrators for those churches or pious institutions which by law or by the documents of foundation do not have an administrator.

> In addition to the diocesan council of administration, in the administration of goods belonging to a church or a pious place which does not, under

[15] *Concil. Plen. Austral. IV,* decr. no. 655.

[16] Canon 1520, §§ 2, 3, 4.

[17] Cf. canon 11.

[18] Cf. Vermeersch-Creusen, *Epitome,* II, n. 841, as against Coronata, *Institutiones,* II, no. 1061, p. 474.

> the law or the articles of its foundation, have its own administrator, the ordinary shall appoint far-seeing, suitable men of good reputation, whom, at the lapse of a three-year term, he shall replace with others, unless local circumstances indicate a contrary course in respect to their term of office.[19]

It is to be noted that the law specifies certain qualifications for the appointees. These are foresight, suitability and good reputation. The insistence upon these qualifications is but a reiteration of the high standards set by Clement V[20] and continued in the Tridentine legislation.[21] Hence these administrators must possess prudence, discretion and that necessary business acumen, tempered with caution, which will urge them to appreciate the worthwhile plans and suggestions of those associates with whom they must deal in their administration of church property. Needless to say, their reputation must be such that the ordinary has moral certainty that they will not yield to avarice, carelessness or extravagance in the execution of their office. While the duration of their appointment is three years, any good reason suffices for the ordinary to retain them for a longer period. The sole judge of what constitutes a good reason in view of local circumstances is the ordinary.

The IV Plenary Council urges that administrators of ecclesiastical goods, whether they be pastors or others, administer the property entrusted to them with the same diligence as a good head of a family administers his own goods.[22] As the Church is ever solicitous for the security and improvement of its property, there is a natural preference for clerics to administer its temporal goods. Nevertheless, the Church is also cognizant of the fact that greater financial and legal acumen, or the fulfilllment of the terms of a will, often furnishes a reason for the appointment of laymen to help in their administration. In this respect,

[19] Canon 1521, § 1.

[20] Cf. c. 2, *de religiosis domibus, ut episcopo sint subiectae*, III, in Clem.

[21] Conc. Trident., sess. VII, *de ref.*, c. 15; sess. XXV, *de ref.*, c. 8.

[22] *Concil. Plen. Austral. IV*, decr. 656.

however, they are only helpers or sharers in the work, and cannot be placed in the sole control of ecclesiastical property.[23]

> But if laymen share in the administration of ecclesiastical property either in virtue of the lawful terms of a foundation, or under a title granted in the act of establishment, or through the wish of the local ordinary, nevertheless the entire administration shall be carried on in the name of the Church and without prejudice to the right of the ordinary to make an inspection, to demand an accounting, and to prescribe the method of administration.[24]

The provisions of canon 1521 are applicable to cases in which neither the law nor the foundation charter has singled out anyone to act as an administrator.[25] Hence it is to be noted that, inasmuch as a pastor is, *ipso iure,* the administrator of the parish entrusted to him, canon 1521 does not require the local ordinary to appoint church committeemen to assist him in the administration. Whenever laymen have a share in the administration, they must render an account of it to the local ordinary. This must be done once a year according to the ruling of canon 1525, § 1, and also in line with decree no. 655 of the IV Plenary Council.

Article 3. The Duty of General and Special Administrators

The duties of specially appointed administrators are set forth in canon 1522, and the general duties of administrators in canons 1523-1528, while the IV Plenary Council devotes seven decrees to matters which relate to general and special administrators.

> Before the administrators of ecclesiastical goods who receive mention in canon 1521 assume their office:
>
> 1. They must give assurance, through an oath

[23] Cf. Coronata, *Institutiones,* II, no. 1062, p. 475.

[24] Canon 1521, § 2.

[25] The law frequently provides for administrators. Cf. canons 1182 ff. 1476 ff., 1489, § 3. See Abbo-Hannan, *The Sacred Canons,* II, 451 ff., 688 ff., 700 ff.

> taken in the presence of the local ordinary or the vicar forane, that they will efficiently and faithfully carry on their work of administration;
> 2. There shall be made an accurate itemized inventory, which all shall sign, of the immovable property and of the precious and other movable property, with a description of it and an estimate of its value; or a previously made inventory shall be accepted, with a notation of the property that has been acquired or lost since it was made.
> 3. One copy of this inventory shall be filed in the archives of the local administration, and another in the archives of the curia; and in both there shall be noted whatever change may happen to affect the status of the property involved.[26]

The drawing up of accurate and itemized inventories, both by the bishop himself and by lesser administrators for the various classes of church property is inculcated many times throughout the Code.[27]

> The administrators of ecclesiastical property are required to fulfill their responsibility with the diligence of a good family head; hence they must:
> 1. Exercise vigilance that the property entrusted to their care shall not be destroyed or damaged;
> 2. Observe the requirements of both canan law and civil law, as well as those which were specified by the founder or the donor, or imposed by legitimate authority;
> 3. Collect promptly and in full all income and profits, safeguard them, and distribute them in accordance with the intention of the founder or with established laws or norms;
> 4. With the consent of the ordinary, invest for the benefit of the church itself the money of the church which is left over and above expenses, and which can be thus profitably employed;
> 5. Keep the books of receipts and expenditure well audited;
> 6. Correctly draw up and file in the archives, or in a suitable and adequate safe belonging to the church, the documents and title deeds on which

[26] Canon 1522.

[27] Cf. canons 1296, § 2; 1299, § 3; 1300; and 1483, § 3. Cf. also *Concil. Plen. Austral. IV*, decr. 659, 660.

> the rights of the church are based; and, where it can conveniently be done, deposit authentic copies of them in the archive or safe of the curia.[28]

The regulations stated in canon 1523 are binding on pastors in virtue of canon 1182, § 1, and on church committeemen in virtue of canons 1184 and 1522. Furthermore, the IV Plenary Council specifically requires insurance, which should include in all cases adequate fire insurance and, in those areas, which are subject to hurricanes or cyclones, adequate storm or flood coverage.

> Churches, schools, presbyteries and other ecclesiastical buildings, if any, should be protected against losses and insured with some insurance company approved by the ordinary.[29]
>
> If Catholic insurance companies are available, they are preferably to be patronized, whenever in other respects the considerations remain equal.[30]

It seems since, at the present time, the number of parishes has grown to large proportions with the consequent multiplication of churches, schools, ecclesiastical buildings and other institutions, that a diocese itself, or at least a province on a co-operative basis, could establish its own insurance company. It would have no other interest than diocesan affairs. During the initial stages of development excessive risks or a part thereof could be underwritten by an outside insurance corporation, e.g., Lloyds of London, at a determined premium, until the non-profit diocesan or provincial society was of sufficient strength to stand alone. The consequent saving accruing to each and every parish and ecclesiastical institution would more than justify the initial endeavour, while the society itself, once firmly established, would provide solid backing for other financial commitments of the diocese.

> In all parishes an inventory of all parochial goods is to be made, signed by the pastor himself and lodged in the parochial archives. An authentic copy is to be placed in the diocesan curia.[31]

[28] Canon 1523, 1°-6°.

[29] *Concil. Plen. Austral. IV*, decr. n. 657.

[30] *Ibid.*, decr. n. 658.

[31] *Ibid.*, decr. n. 659.

> In the inventories all goods, both movable and immovable, which belong to the church, school, cemetery and presbytery, and especially the permanent income, if any, and the debts to which the the parish is subjected, must be itemized.[32]
> When a new pastor takes over a parish the inventory is to be examined, and what has been lost or acquired is to be noted.[33]
> Unless the parish had been vacated through death, the former pastor is obliged to assist at this examination, to give an account and to sign the acts.[34]

It follows as a corollary from these decrees that every pastor should clearly mark what are his own personal effects, lest, in the course of the years, they become identified with any of the movable church property in use at the rectory. To obviate recriminations and hard feelings, and perhaps even legal action by his beneficiaries, if not also the jeopardy occasioned for the safety of the church property itself, this is a just and a practical procedure.

Canon 1524 explicitly applies the fundamental principles of social justice that should motivate not only clerics, religious and administrators of Church property, but indeed all Christians in the just and honorable treatment of their employees.

> All, especially clerics, religious, and the administrators of ecclesiastical property shall, in contracts of hire, provide employees with an honorable and just wage; they shall arrange opportunity for the latter to devote a suitable period of time to piety; on no account shall they through miserliness withdraw the employees from the care of their family or burden them with a load of work that transcends their physical capacity, or with a kind of work to which their age or sex is not suited.[35]

Only through the strict observance of the spirit and letter of this canon is it possible that the evils of social

[32] *Ibid.*, decr. n. 660.
[33] *Ibid.*, decr. n. 661.
[34] *Ibid.*, decr. n. 662.
[35] Canon 1524.

injustice be avoided. In the present decade, indeed, in consequence of the highly organized condition and efficiency of trade unions, there may be little chance of violating the present law. Nevertheless, it behooves all administrators of every class of ecclesiastical institution faithfully to observe the spirit of Christian justice and charity. Even in individual and isolated cases must they remember that "the laborer is worthy of his hire."[36]

The principles enunciated by Leo XIII,[37] the present law of the Church as stated in this canon, and its clarification and application in the writings of Pius XI[38] leave no doubt about the importance and gravity of this canon. It is to be noted that an honorable and just wage is to be computed as one that proves sufficient for a family, and not merely for an individual worker.[39] The obligation of paying a just wage, one that is adequate for the reasonable and frugal comfort of a family of five, is considered by commentators as imposed on all at least by the positive law of the Church, if not also by the natural law.[40]

> 1. Both ecclesiastical and lay administrators of any church, including the cathedral church, or of a canonically established pious place or confraternity, are bound by their office to render an account once a year to the ordinary of the place, without any regard to contrary custom; such custom the the law completely reprobates.
>
> 2. If by a particular law an account must also be rendered to others specifically designated, then the local ordinary or his delegate must be included among these, and an exoneration from this obliga-

[36] Luke, X:7.

[37] Litt. encycl. *Rerum novarum,* 15 maii 1891, n. 32—*Fontes,* III, n. 611, pp. 355 ff.

[38] Litt. encycl. *Quadragesimo anno,* 15 maii 1931—*AAS,* XXIII (1931), 177 ff.; 199.

[39] Cf. litt. encycl. *Casti connubii,* 31 dec. 1930—*AAS,* XXII (1930), 539 ff.; 586.

[40] Cf. H. Noldin-A. Schmitt, *Summa Theologia Moralis iuxta Codicem Iuris Canonici* (24. ed., 3 vols., Ratisbonae: F. Puset, 1936), II, nos. 610 ff., pp. 551 ff.; Vermeersch-Creusen, *Epitome,* II, n. 484.

[41] Canon 1535, § 1, § 2.

> tion is of absolutely no juridical value to the administrators.[41]

It is to be noted that all contrary customs whatsoever, even immemorial customs, whether univerisal or particular, are abrogated.[42] The churches, pious places and confraternities, however, which receive mention in this canon are such only as are subject to the authority of the ordinary.[43] Hence churches and property belonging to exempt religious, or enjoying a special privilege of exemption, are not subject to the ruling of this canon,[44] while, on the contrary, the administrators of churches entrusted to religious, although *pleno iure* attached to a monastery, are not exempted.[45]

The IV Plenary Council specifically requires administrators accurately to keep the books of receipts and expenses according to the method suggested by the ordinary. The auditor mentioned in the decree must be a reputable and qualified one, and not merely some willing parishioner who, lacking a diploma in accountancy, may or may not be skilled in helping the pastor keep the parochial accounts.

> Administrators are obliged accurately to keep the the books of receipts and expenditure according to instructions given by the ordinary. These books are to be examined and approved by an auditor once a year. In the month specified by the curia the administrators are to submit the report to the ordinary for approval.[46]

The decrees of the IV Plenary Council do not reflect any restriction or extension of the Church's law regarding the requisite permission for the entering of law suits.

> Administrators shall not enter suit or a defense to a suit in the name of the Church, unless they shall have obtained the written permission from the local ordinary or at least, in a case of emergency, from the vicar forane, who shall then im-

[42] Cf. canon 5.

[43] Cf. canon 1519, § 1.

[44] Cf. canon 615.

[45] Cf. *Concil. Plen. Austral. IV*, decr. no. 664; supra, p. 75.

[46] *Concil. Plen. Austral. IV*, decr. 663.

> mediately inform the ordinary of the permission given.[47]

Administrators, therefore, shall be neither a plaintiff nor a defendant in a suit at law without the necessary permission. This prohibition is applicable even in the case of a suit in an ecclesiastical court.[48] By the term *church* is understood in this instance any collegiate or non-collegiate moral personality in the Church.[49]

> 1. Administrators act invalidly in performing acts that exceed the limits or the method of ordinary administration, unless they have previously obtained the written authority of the local ordinary.
>
> 2. The church is not responsible for contracts entered into by administrators who lacked the permission of a competent superior, except when, and to the extent to which, it has profited from them.[50]

What constitutes acts of ordinary and extraordinary administration has been treated earlier.[51] These acts which exceed the limits of ordinary administration are each and every act of alienation,[52] the investment of capital, the opening of a cemetery, the establishment of a school or similar institution, and the taking up of special collections.[53]

The IV Fourth Plenary Council specifically requires that all administrators, except in matters of lesser importance, must have the written permission of the competent ecclesiastical authority before proceeding to sell, exchange, or lease out ecclesiastical goods. Otherwise they act invalidly.[54]

Furthermore, the administrator who contracts

[47] Canon 1526.

[48] Cf. Abbo-Hannan, *The Sacred Canons*, II, 730.

[49] Cf. canons 99; 100, § 1.

[50] Canon 1526, § 1, § 2.

[51] Cf. *supra*, p. 75.

[52] Cf. Chapter V.

[53] Cf. S.C. de Prop. Fide, 21 iul. 1856—*Coll. S.C.P.F.*, no. 1127; *Fontes*, no. 4841.

[54] Cf. *Concil. Plen. Austral. IV*, decr. no. 664; supra, p. 75.

> debts without the written permission of the ordinary is himself held responsible.[55]
>
> When, on the contrary, debts are contracted with the permission of the ordinary, they are to be undertaken in the name of the trustees of the church property.[56]
>
> Even though they be held to their administration neither by the title of a benefice nor by the title of an ecclesiastical office, administrators who on their own authority abandon the charge which they expressly or tacitly accepted, with resulting injury to the church, are bound to make restitution.[57]

The reason is that, when an administrator assumes a charge of administration, there is an implied or tacit contract in virtue of which he is obliged, as far as lies in his power, to avert losses to the church.[58]

[55] Ibid., decr. no. 665.
[56] *Ibid.*, decr. no. 676.
[57] Canon 1528.
[58] Cf. Beste, *Introductio in Codicem*, p. 761.

CHAPTER V

ALIENATION OF ECCLESIASTICAL GOODS

ARTICLE 1. CONTRACTS IN CANON AND CIVIL LAW

Contracts, pacts or agreements[1] are the principal transmissive means by which the Church acquires temporal goods. Most of the acts of its administration of temporal goods, wherever there is need and especially in matters requiring the alienation of property, the Church carries out by means of contracts.[2] A contract is an agreement, manifested in some visible fashion, between two or more persons, about an object which as acceptable to both gives rise to an obligation for at least one of the contracting parties.[3]

Contracts are variously classified. They are called:

1. *Unilateral,* when they give rise to an obligation in only one of the contracting parties, e.g., a promise or a gift; or *bilateral,* when they produce an obligation in each of the contracting parties, e.g., a contract of buying or selling.
2. *Consenual,* when they are essentially perfected by the consent alone with the parties, or *real,* when the contract necessitates the handing over of the goods, e.g., a loan or a pledge.
3. *Gratuitous* or *onerous,* in so far as liability is intended by one of the parties and extended to the other, or the contract imposes a burden on each of them.
4. *Formally expressed* (*formaliter initi*), when by suitable words or signs the agreement is signi-

[1] The terms pacts, contracts, stipulations, which were distinguishable in Roman Law, are now used more or less indiscriminately. Cf. Noldin, *Summa Theologiae Moralis,* II, n. 523.

[2] Cf. Wernz-Vidal, *Ius Canonicum,* IV, Pars II, n. 844.

[3] Beste, *op. cit.,* p. 761. Cf. Noldin, *op. cit.,* II, no. 523; Dominicus M. Prümmer, *Manuale Theologiae Moralis* (10. ed., 3 vols., Barcelona: Editoral Herder, 1945), II, 211 ff.; Aloysius Sabetti-Timotheus Barrett, *Compendium Theologiae Moralis* (editio XXIX, Neo Eboraci: Frederick Pustet Co. Inc., 1920), pp. 419 ff.

fied, or *implied* (or *quasi-contract*), when through the assmuption of one obligation other obligations necessarily follow from the nature of the agreement, e.g., the acceptance of an office, which implicitly brings with it the obligation of fulfilling its duties. Hence the assumption of the office evinces a *quasi-contract*.

5. *Nominate,* that is, named contracts or contracts of a determined character, and *innominate,* that is, unnamed contracts or contracts of an indeterminate nature, in so far as they have their own proper name or are designated by a special name. Unnamed contracts lack their own special name. These contracts are of four kinds, viz., *do ut des, do ut facias, facio ut des, facio ut facias.* Moral thologians treat of these contracts at great length.[4]

In civil law a valid contract is an agreement made between two or more parties, whereby legal obligations are created which the law will enforce. Certain formalities must necessarily be observed in order that rights may be acquired and obligations incurred. These formalities are called the *essential elements.* Apart from the presence of all of the elements the contract will be invalid. These elements are:

1. The *intention* of the parties to create a legal relationship.
2. The offer by one party and its *acceptance* by the other.
3. The *form* or *valuable consideration.*
4. *The legal capacity* of the parties to act.
5. The *genuine consent* by the parties.
6. The *legality* of the objects of the agreement.[5]

Agreements which are binding at law are termed contracts. It should be noted, however, that not all agreements are contracts. Contracts are only those agreements for which the law authorizes permission and assistance, which are entered into by two or more persons, with one promis-

[4] Beste, *op. cit.,* p. 761. Noldin, *op. cit.,* II, no. 524.

[5] Robert Keith Yorston and Edward E. Fortesque, *Australian Mercantile Law* (8. ed., Sydney: The Law Book Co. of Australasia Pty. Ltd., 1955), pp. 10 ff.

ing to another, or with two persons promising to one another, to do or to refrain from doing some specified act or acts. Hence, in order to be a contract, the agreement must create legal obligations. In some cases the contract or the evidence of it must exist in a prescribed form, i.e., in writing or by deed. From a legal viewpoint, however, it is not necessary that all contracts be in writing. Likewise a contract may exist without written evidence. As a result these latter contracts, provided that the conditions mentioned above are present, are enforceable at law.[6]

As in moral theology and canon law, so also in civil law, contracts are variously classified. The main classification is into *formal* and *simple* contracts. A *formal contract* is one that is expressed in a special manner to which the law gives particular effect, and by *consideration* reference is made to some gain or benefit accruing to the party making the promise.[7]

Formal contracts are of two kinds:

(a) *Contract of record*, entered into through the machinery of a court of justice, e.g., a judgment or a recognizance (a bale or bail-bond).

(b) *Specialty contracts*, by deed, i.e., by writing, sealed and delivered. Such contracts obtain their binding force from their form alone. It is not always essential that a seal be actually affixed, for it suffices that the contract is designated as a deed.[8] Every deed, however, must now be signed[9] and attested by at least one witness who is not a party to the deed.

Simple or *parol contracts* are contracts in writing other than by a deed, or also verbal contracts.[10] The important

[6] The law requiring at least a written memorandum for certain contracts is based on 29 Charles 11, chap. 3 (1677-78), called "*The Statute of Frauds.*"

[7] Yorston and Fortesque, *op. cit.*, p. 24.

[8] *Ibid.*, p. 25.

[9] New South Wales—*Conveyancying Acts 1919-1953*, S.38(1).

[10] Robert Keith Yorston, *The Australian Commercial Dictionary* (2. ed., Sydney: The Law Book Co. of Australasia Pty Ltd., 1950), p. 93.

essential in all simple contracts is that a *valuable consideration* must be present for their validity. A *valuable consideration* in the sense of the law "may consist either in some right, interest, profit, or benefit accruing to one party, or some forbearance,[11] detriment, loss or responsibility given, suffered or undertaken by the other."[12] It is whatever is done or suffered, or promised to be done or suffered, by one party in return for, and in respect of, the promise of the other party.[13]

Contracts may be *expressed* or *implied*. An *expressed contract* is one in which the contract is formulated by words, written or spoken. An *implied contract* is one in which the agreement is reached, not by words, written or spoken, but by the acts or conduct of the parties. A *quasi-contract* differs from an implied contract in that the former is an obligation imposed by law, regardless of any agreement or wishes of the parties concerned.[14]

A contract may be:

1. *Valid*—one which the law will enforce.
2. *Void*—one which is of no legal effect between the parties, and thus does not create legal rights or obligations, e.g., a contract to commit a crime.
3. *Voidable*—one which is capable of being disclaimed at the option of one of the parties, e.g., a contract wherein the assent of one party is obtained by means of fraud.
4. *Unenforceable*—one which in itself is valid, but because of some technical defect is not capable of being enforced, e.g., a verbally made contract which is required by statute to be evidenced in writing.

To be valid, the following contracts are required to be in writing:

(i) Bills of exchange, cheques and promissory

[11] *Forbearance.* To abstain or refrain from doing. The giving up of a right may constitute a consideration. Refraining from exercising a right is frequently the consideration in case of compromise.

[12] *Currie* v. *Misa* (1875) L.R. 10 Ex. 162.

[13] Yorston and Fortesque, *op. cit.*, 28.

[14] Cf. Yorston and Fortesque, *op. cit.*, 12.

notes. (Bills of Exchange Act [Commonwealth]).

(ii) Assignments of copyright. (Copyright Act [Commonwealth]).

(iii) A transfer of shares in a company (except in Tasmania).

(iv) Submission to arbitration in the sense that the parties thereto are not bound by the various State Arbitration Acts unless the submission is in writing.

In addition the following contracts are required to be *evidenced in writing* before they become enforceable:

(i) Contracts whereby an executor or an administrator promises to satisfy the liability of a deceased person out of his own money.

(ii) Contracts of guarantee or suretyship, but not contracts of indemnity.[15]

(iii) Agreements made in consideration of marriage.

(iv) Agreements not to be performed within one year from the making thereof.

(v) Contracts for the sale of land or other disposition of land, or any interest in land.

The following contracts are required, for validity, to be *by deed*:

(i) a gratuitous promise, i.e., a promise for which the promisor receives no consideration to support his promise.

(ii) Contracts entered into by corporations aggregate, except:

(a) those which deal with trifling matters or matters of daily occurrence, and

(b) those which, inasmuch as then can be made by parol can similarly be made by parol on behalf of the corporation by any person acting under its authority expressed or implied.

(iii) Appointment of an agent where he is given authority to contract by deed (called a POWER OF ATTORNEY).

[15] Cf. canon 137.

(iv) A lease of land for a period exceeding three years.[16]

Since by and large in English-speaking countries Catholics are in the minority, it is but natural that the Church, when it does have contact with the civil law, will deal with people outside the fold. Indeed, it is in the field of contracts that the Church and its members will have most contact with the civil law. And since such contracts so frequently become matters of dispute before the civil law, the Church does its utmost to avoid conflicts with lay courts. It has no desire to encroach, or indeed even to create the impression of encroaching, upon state rights. Hence to lessen the danger of harmful opposition to and from the civil authority, it has sought out for contracts some common juridical ground whereon all parties may meet on an equal footing. Long before the promulgation of the present Code of Canon Law the first three Plenary Councils of Australia made provision for the holding of ecclesiastical property according to the civil law of the state wherein the property was located.[17]

This legislation was in accord with the ruling of the Sacred Congregation for the Propagation of the Faith in a decree of December 15, 1840, whereby all bishops and religious superiors in the United States of America were ordered to provide for the proper and legal transfer of Church property to their successors by making wills *"iuxta legem staus, in quo degunt, quarum accuratam notitiam ex certis fontibus sibi comparabunt."*[18]

The present law of the Church in canon 1529 canonizes the secular law in the matter of contracts:

> What the secular law of the territory provides in the matter of contracts, generally and specifically, whether in named or unnamed contracts, and concerning payments, shall be observed as enacted by canon law in ecclesiastical matters with the same

[16] Yorston, *The Australian Commercial Dictionary*, pp. 93, 94.

[17] Cf. *Council. Plen. Aust. I, 1885*, decr. n. 271; *Concil. Plen. Aust. II, 1895*, decr. n. 341; *Concil. Plen. Aust. III, 1905*, decr. n. 368.

[18] *Coll. S.C.P.F.*, n. 916.

effects, unless it is contrary to the divine law or unless other provision is made by the canon law[19]

While the New South Wales law makes no distinction between named and unnamed contracts, it does recognize both implied and quasi-contracts.[20]

ARTICLE 2. THE NATURE OF ALIENATION AND ITS REQUISITE CONDITIONS

A. THE NATURE OF ALIENATION

The word *"alienation"* is derived from the Latin *alienare,* to make something belong to another. Hence, etymologically, it means making something become the property of another. Considered juridically, it implies the transfer of the direct ownership of an object to another, whether by sale or exchange, i.e., for some consideration, or gratuitously, as by a gift or donation. In its strict meaning, alienation[21] involves only those acts and contracts by which some temporal property passes directly from the ownership of any actual or moral person by any method or title to the ownership of another person.[22] In its broad sense, however, alienation involves every transaction in which ownership is even diminished without being given up entirely, or in which the Church is exposed to the juridical danger of losing or lessening its proprietary rights over goods possessed.[23]

Hence, in the canons that follow, the Code applies the term "alienation" to *mortgages,*[24] which confer on another a conditional right to church property; to the *contracting of debts,* for thereby administrators of ecclesiastical goods

[19] Canon 1529.

[20] Cf. Yorston and Fortesque, *Australian Mercantile Law,* p. 12.

[21] *Proprie dicta* cf. canon 1533.

[22] Cf. Beste, *Introductio in Codicem,* p. 761.

[23] Edward Louis Heston, *The Alienation of Church Propterty in The United States,* The Catholic University of America Canon Law Studies, no. 132 (Washington D.C.: The Catholic University of America Press, 1941), p. 70.

[24] Cf. canon 1542.

are limited and restricted in the use of rights consequent upon ownership; to *leases and rentals*[25] when they extend for a period of time longer than nine years, for thereby the Church is similarly restricted in the complete use and ownership of its property; to the allowing of *passive easements* or *servitudes*, or the renunciation of *active easements* or *servitudes*, since these either confer on another a right to use church property or to deprive the Church of a right already acquired; to *compromise* and *yielding lawsuits*, whereby the Church agrees to a diminution of its objective rights in order to avoid publicized lawsuits and to maintain harmony and goodwill. Likewise to *pledge* ecclesiastical goods or to use them as *surety* for others would be tantamount to alienation in this wide sense, for such actions place the goods under the potential ownership of others and add a further liability that diminishes the value of property already owned.[26] In short, alienation in this broad sense includes all acts or contracts whereby the proprietary rights of the Church are legally jeopardized.[27]

In matter concerning alienation the Church cannot afford to be a respecter of persons. The best interests of the Church are always to be protected and furthered . Hence it is that the more valuable the property to be alienated, or the greater the amount that is jeopardized, the more serious the reason and the urgency that are required, and the greater the authority that is demanded in whatever superior grants the permission. In most cases it is the Holy See itself. Without the restraining hand of general legislation, ordinaries and religious superiors in general could be too easily and too quickly led into transactions which

[25] Cf. canons 1541, 1479.

[26] Heston, *op. cit.*, p. 70.

[27] This wide interpretation is expressly stressed in a letter sent by the Apostolic Delegate in the United States to all religious superiors: "The term *alienation* includes not only purchases or transfers of property, but includes as well any contract, debt or obligation. The Canon Law regards all transactions, which may render the financial condition of the Institute, Province or religious house less secure, as alienations."—Bouscaren, *Canon Law Digest*, II, 162.

might endanger the security and the best interests of the property under their charge.[28]

The ecclesiastical goods which are the object of the law with regard to alienation are to be understood as those goods which are owned by some ecclesiastical moral person according to the definition given in canon 1497, § 1, namely, temporal property, both movable and immovable, and other property, whether corporeal or incorporeal, which belongs either to the Apostolic See or to some other moral person in the Church. It is to be noted that not every transaction in which administrators are involved is to be regarded as alienation.

One must distinguish between the use of *capital assets* or *stable capital* and the ordinary working capital or funds which are received and expended in the course of the operation and administration of any ecclesiastical moral person. *Capital assets* or *stable capital*, or in the traditional ecclesiastical language the *patrimony* of a church, includes all those assets which are not in ordinary circulation but serve to constitute the permanent basis of an ecclesiastical moral person's financial security. "It is that sum which has been legitimately set aside to remain intact and be a source of regular income."[29]

Hence, stable capital consists of deposits at interest in a bank, in contradistinction to deposits in a current cheque account for operating expenses; in interest-bearing securities, stocks or bonds; in property rented or leased by the church, etc. It is when these capital assets are diminished or legally jeopardized in any way that alienation in the canonical sense occurs. It should be noted, however, that income by the very fact of its being acquired is not thereby automatically incorporated in the stable capital. Once, how-

[28] "Ratio huius tam multiplicis prohibitionis est necessitas, et utilitas ecclesiarum et locorum piorum, contra quam praelati, aliique administratores facile alienationes fecissent, nisi hae adeo multiplici, et stricta lege fuissent prohibitae." Schmalzgrueber, *Ius Ecclesiasticum Universum*, Lib. III, tit. 13, n. 26.

[29] Heston, *op. cit.*, p. 73.

ever, the money has been formally invested or placed permanently at interest in the bank, it is surely aggregated to the fixed assets of the ecclesiastical corporation, and is thus an integral part of the stable capital.

B. THE REQUISITE CONDITIONS FOR ALIENATION

> 1. With due regard to the ruling of canon 1281, § 1, for the alienation of non-perishable ecclesiastical property, whether movable or immovable, there is acquired:
>
> 1°. A written appraisal of the property made by approved experts;
>
> 2°. A justifying reason, i.e., urgent need, or the evident advantage to the Church, or piety;
>
> 3°. The permission of the lawful superior, in the absence of which the alienation is invalid.
>
> 2. Other opportune precautions which serve to prevent loss to the Church are not to be omitted, but are to be specified by the respective superior according to the circumstances of the case.[30]

Canon 1281, § 1, requires the permission of the Apostolic See for the valid alienation or transfer of images and relics of great importance.[31] In this and the following canons the property in question, both movable and immovable is such that in character it is non-perishable (*bona quae servando servari possunt*).

The first condition for the lawful alienation of church goods is that they should be evaluated by experts. Since the wording of the law employs the plural, *a probis peritis*, at least two independent opinions are needed for a sufficient appraisal. The written appraisal of each may be submitted separately.[32] It should be noted that in Australia the Valuer General's estimate should not be included as that of one of the two skilled assessors. The Valuer Gener-

[30] Canon 1530, §§ 1, 2.

[31] C. 37, D. 1, *de cons.;* c. 2, X, *de reliquiis et veneratione sanctorum*, III, 45.

[32] Cf. A. Blat, *Commentarium Textus Codicis Iuris Canonici* (5 vols. in 6, Romae: Ex Typographia Pontificia in Instituto Pii IX, 1919-27), III, pars VI, no. 446.

al's official estimate, rated for taxation purposes, does not always reveal the actual current value. Furthermore, it is subject to such infrequent and unperiodic revision as to be very misleading to the unwary vendor or purchaser. The purpose of this appraisal by experts is obviously the protection of the Church against unscrupulous bargainers, and also against the inexperience and even imprudence of administrators of ecclesiastical property. Hence, the appraisal should take into account not only the present condition of a given area, but also the potential of the district in view of scheduled works or improvements to be made there.

The second condition for lawful alienation is a justfying necessity may be one or another of three kinds:

(a) Urgent necessity, i.e., the actual need that there and then the transaction be performed for the avoidance of spiritual or material loss, e.g., the repair of a church after a fire or a flood;

(b) Evident utility, i.e., not merely a probable but rather a reasonably evident advantage accruing to the Church from the fact of alienation;

(c) Piety, i.e., any work of charity or benevolence, spiritual or corporal, that would follow from the alienation, e.g., the building of a school, church or hospital.

The third condition is the authorization of the legitimate superior. This permission, furthermore, according to the law, is explicitly required for the validity of all alienations. The IV Plenary Council of Australia, however, makes an exception in matters of lesser importance,[33] but reiterates that if the requisite permission is not obtained the transaction will be invalid. Hence, it may be noted that the first two conditions, an appraisal by experts made in writing and a justifying necessity, are required, not for the valid but simply for the lawful alienation. This differs from the pre-

[33] Cf.*Concil. Plen. Austral. IV*, decr. 664.

Code legislation, which required a just cause for the validity of every alienation.[34]

The second section of canon 1530 implicitly exhorts ordinaries and other superiors to make suitable provisions for their territories and subjects according as prudence and necessity may suggest. These regulations and opportune precautions should prescribe the manner of asking for permission, the formalities to be observed, and the details that are important for the welfare of the ecclesiastical corporation entrusted to their care and vigilance.

ARTICLE 3. THE MANNER OF ALIENATION

> 1. A thing shall not be alienated for a price less than that specified in the estimate.
>
> 2. The alienation shall be carried out by way of public auction or at least public notice of it shall be served, unless circumstances suggest a different course; and the thing shall be sold to him who, all things considered, offered the highest bid.
>
> 3. The money received from the alienation shall be carefully, securely and advantageously invested for the benefit of the Church.[35]

The first provision in canon 1531 follows naturally upon the prescript incorporated in canon 1530, § 1. Its reasonableness is evident, since it would be useless to have the property appraised only to see the estimate disregarded in an actual sale. Nevertheless, if the appraisers' set price is not reached, other opinions should be sought in settlement upon a reasonable price as safeguarding the best interests of the Church. Only in cases of extreme and grave necessity should a price lower than the smallest estimate of many appraisers be accepted.

Public auction or, at least, advertisement is ordinarily the best and soundest method of achieving a price compatible with current standards. Competition usually produces the highest bidder with advantageous results to the

[34] Cf. Schmalzgrueber, *op. cit.* Lib. III, tit. 13, nn. 69-70. De Meester, *Compendium,* III, no. 1485.

[35] Canon 1531, §§ 1, 2, 3.

vendor. To prevent loss to the Church and to offset any collusion among prospective buyers, the administrators should set a reserve price, preferably the lowest of the appraisers' estimates, so that upon any lower bid the auctioneer will pass the property back to the owner, i.e., to the Church, without a sale. The prescriptions of the civil law in Australia are, according to canon 1529, the canon law for such sales.[36]

It is to be observed, also, that other considerations may persuade an administrator to accept a price lower than the highest offer made. It could happen that harm or loss would accrue to the Church in other ways if a hostile purchaser took over the property. The non-observance of the requisites of this canon does not affect the validity of the transaction.[37]

The use of the proceeds of the alienation is regulated in § 3 of canon 1531, i.e., the money received from the sale must be invested in a manner which is safe, secure and useful. Ordinarily the proceeds should be used for the reintegration of the fixed capital in a manner proportionate to its depletion in consequence of the alienation. As was seen in the previous canon,[38] when the Church authorizes alienation, it requires that opportune precautions for the prevention of harm and loss be observed. The IV Plenary Council further requires that before the re-investment of such money the permission of the ordinary be obtained on each and every occasion.

> Without the permission of the ordinary, which must be obtained on each occasion, a priest may not invest the money of the church in immovable goods or in securities or stocks. Otherwise he is held responsible for the damages that perhaps will arise.[39]

Hence, a twofold permission is needed if a pastor wishes to dispose of superfluous property and to make a re-invest-

[36] Cf. canon 1529.

[37] Cf. Augustine, *A Commentary on the new Code of Canon Law*, VI, 596.

[38] Canon 1530, § 2.

[39] *Concil. Plen. Austral. IV*, decr. 679.

ment in other land or property, or in bonds. He needs permission: (a) to alienate the property in the first place,[40] and (b) to re-invest the payment for it in immovable goods or securities or stocks.[41]

Canon 1532 specifies the particular application of the principle enunciated in canon 1530, § 1, 3°, namely the permission of the legitimate superior which is required and without which alienation is invalid. It should be noted that, as canon 534 regulates this same matter for religious communities, this present canon applies only to the secular clergy.

> 1. The lawful superior as mentioned in canon 1530, § 1, 3°, is the Apostolic See if the property involved is:
> 1°. A precious object;
> 2°. Objects whose value exceeds 30,000 lire or francs.[42]

The respective fields of competence of the Roman Congregations are well defined in the particular canons pertaining to their powers. In accord therewith the competent superior for the alienation of precious goods and for all transactions of the secular clergy is the Sacred Congregation of the Council;[43] for the alienation of property held by religious institutes, the Sacred Congregation of Religious;[44] and for the alienation of property in missionary countries, which rule still obtains in Australia, the Sacred Congregation for the Propagation of the Faith.[45] Hence, when the Apostolic See is referred to in the matter of alienation, one or the other of the above mentioned Congregations is indicated.

What constitutes an object as *precious* has already been shown.[46] There is was seen than an object worth less than

[40] Cf. *ibid.*, decr. 664; also canon 1530, § 1, 3°.
[41] *Ibid.*, decr. 679.
[42] Canon 1532, § 1, 1°, 2°.
[43] Cf. canon 250, § 2.
[44] Canons 251, § 1; 676, § 2.
[45] Cf. canon 252, §§ 1, 2.
[46] Cf. canon 1497, § 2; *supra*, p. 26.

100 pounds sterling is not considered precious. Analogous to the category of precious objects is that of votive offerings made at a shrine or an altar,[47] and that of the major (*insignes*) relics of the saints.[48]

The value of the 30,000 lire or francs mentioned in canon 1532, § 1, 2°, should be understood of their gold value as computable at the time of the promulgation of the Code.[49] At that time 1000 francs equalled about forty pounds sterling. Until 1931, apart from the cost of exchange if that was necessary, there was no appreciable difference between the pound sterling and the Australian pound.[50] Hence 30,000

[47] Cf. S.C.C. resp. Jan. 14, 1922 (AAS., XIV, 160; Bouscaren, *op. cit.*, 1, 730.

[48] Cf. S.C.C., resol. 13 iul. 1919—*AAS.*, XI (1919), 416; Bouscaren, *Canon Law Digest*, 1. 729.

[49] Cf. De Meester, *Compendium*, III, no. 1487. Cf. the letter of the Sacred Congregation for Religious sent to religious superiors in the United States by the Apostolic Delegate on Nov. 13, 1936. "The aforesaid sum of six thousand dollars should be understood, in connection with the terms of the Code, as the equivalent of 'thirty thousand lire or francs' and in reference to the value of currency based upon gold in distinction to other currencies, gold coin being the true unit of value. In this connection the value is based upon stable gold content and rate of exchange."—Bouscaren, *op. cit.*, II, 163.

[50] "The Australian monetary system is based on the British system, of which the unit is the pound (£) divided into 20 shillings (s.) each of 12 pence (d.). When the Australian currency was introduced in 1909, the Australian pound was specified as equivalent to 123.27447 grains of gold 11/12ths fine, or 113.002 grains of fine gold, and until the depression in 1930 was identical with the pound sterling. There was a gradual depreciation of the Australian pound in terms of sterling from the beginning of 1930 until December, 1931, when it was stabilized as the rate of £125 Australian = £100 sterling. This relationship has been maintained until the present time. Following depreciation, no action was taken to define the value of the Australian pound in terms of gold until August, 1947, when the Australian Government advised the International Monetary Fund, in terms of the membership agreement, that the par value of the Australian pound was 2.86507 grammes (44.2148 grains) of fine gold. From September, 1949, this was reduced to 1.99062 grammes (30.720 grains) of fine gold." The Commonwealth Bureau of Census and Statistics, *Year Book of the Commonwealth of Australia* (Government Printer, Canberra, A.C.T. Australia, No. 41, 1955), p. 547.

francs would have been equivalent to 1200 pounds or thereabout until 1930. It seems reasonable, equitable, and indeed the one practicable approach in estimating the relative values to base the solution on the gold value of the respective currencies.

In 1931 the first official depreciation of the Australian pound occurred. This meant that it required 25% more of the latter to equal 30,000 francs gold value, i.e., about 1500 or 1600 pounds. The second depreciation, this time a purely unilateral devaluation with the English pound, took place on September 19, 1949.[51] This elevated the sum beyond which, for purposes of alienation, permission from the Holy See had to be obtained to two thousand pounds, making it more or less equivalent to the purchasing power of $6000.00 in the United States of America, which was the value of 30,000 francs at the time the Code was promulgated.

The Sacred Consistorial Congregation, however, in order to obviate the difficulties that had arisen in various places and to clarify a situation occasioned by inflation and rising costs, issued a decree on July 13, 1951, stating that recourse was to be had to the Apostolic See whenever the sum of money involved in the proposed alienation exceeded 10,000 gold francs or lire.

> Since the changed value of money and the wavering of the currency has occasioned in certain places special difficulties in applying the prescriptions of canons 534, § 1, and 1532, § 1, 2°, of the Code of Canon Law, the Holy See has been asked to issue appropriate regulations.
>
> Wherefore, His Holiness by divine Providence Pope Pius XII, after having carefully considered the matter, has graciously deigned to provide by the present Decree of the Sacred Consistorial Congregation that, while the present conditions continue and at the good pleasure of the Holy See, recourse is to be had to the same Apostolic See

[51] The Commonwealth Bureau of Census and Statistics, *op. cit.*, p. 547.

whenever the sum of money involved exceeds ten thousand gold francs or lire.
Given at Rome, from the Sacred Consistorial Congregation, 13 July, 1951.[52]

Many opinions have been expressed by authors with regard to the value of 30,000 francs or lire.[53] But since the issuance of the decree of the Sacred Consistorial Congregation on July 13, 1951, the question has become more of historical than of practical interest. Whenever the amount involved in the proposed alienation exceeded 10,000 *gold francs* or *lire*, recourse was to be had to the Apostolic See.

It is interesting to note the development of the European currency system, to which apparently the Sacred Congregation has reverted in using the term *gold francs*, or *lire*.[54] The coinage system of France came into force on May 6, 1799. It was extended to the countries forming the Latin Union in 1865, and was adopted by various other countries. "It is the most widely extended system in Europe."

In the latter half of the nineteenth century there was a decided tendency securing, by international action, reforms of monetary systems. "Both by its situation and its currency systems, France was the country that was first led to aim at the establishment of a currency union.... "A preliminary step was the formation of the Latin Union, whereby the currencies of France, Italy, Belgium and Switzerland were, in respect to their gold and silver coins, assimilated."[55]

This seems to explain the use of the words *gold francs* or *lire* when the Sacred Congregation speaks of the 10,000 *gold francs* or *lire* in the 1951 decree. "The unit is the same value all through the union but receives different names in different countries. The titles are: in France, Belgium and

[52] *AAS*, XLIII (1951), 602-603; Bouscaren, *op. cit.*, III, 212.

[53] Cf. Stenger, *The Mortgaging of Church Property*, The Catholic University of America Canon Law Studies, no. 169 (Washington, D.C.: The Catholic University of America Press, 1942), pp. 131-134.

[54] Cf. *Encyclopaedia Britannica* (13. ed., New York: The Encyclopaedia Britannica Inc., 1926), vol. XVIII, pp. 694 ff.

[55] *Ibid.*, p. 706.

Switzerland, *Franc* and *centime;* in Italy, *lira* and *centesimo*. . . ."[56] In point of fact, while currencies have changed considerably, the value of gold itself has not varied since 1935 until the present time; its value or price is still stabilized, despite a world war and a consequent inflation, at $35.00 an ounce.[57] Now the value of gold in a 100 franc piece is 32.258006 grammes of gold of 90% fineness, or 29.032254 grammes of fine gold, that is, .9334 of an ounce of gold.[58] In terms of gold the par value of the Australian pound is £15.625 to one ounce of fine gold.[59] Hence .9334 of £15.625 equals £14.58. Therefore 100 gold francs (of the 1918 vintage) would have a gold content which today would be equivalent to £14.58 Australian currency; or 1000 gold francs would equal £145.8; and 10,000 gold francs or lire, £1458 or, at the current rate of exchange, $3251.34.

These figures, however, are more or less of a purely academic interest, for the Sacred Consistorial Congregation issued a later instruction on October 18, 1952, to the effect that two thousand pounds sterling is the limit beyond which permission has to be sought from the Holy See.

> 1. Until new dispositions are made, which will be communicated by this same Sacred Consistorial Congregation, the sums of money indicated in the following table are to be considered for the respective countries as the limits beyond which the permission of the Holy See is required according to canons 534, § 1, and 1523, § 2, n. 2, of the Code of Canon Law:
>
> | | | |
> |---|---|---|
> | America, North & Central | U.S. Dollars | $5000 |
> | Great Britain | Pounds Sterling | £2000 |
>
> 2. . . . .
>
> 3. By analogy, the sum of "a thousand lire or francs" mentioned in canon 1532, § 2, is to be taken as a sum equal to one-thirtieth of the value indicated in the table.[60]

[56] *Loc. cit.*

[57] Cf. Report, International Monetary Fund, 1956, Washington, D.C.

[58] *Encyclopaedia Britannica,* XVIII, 706.

[59] Report of International Monetary Fund, 1956.

[60] Cf. Bouscaren, *The Canon Law Digest,* Annual Supplement through 1953, under canon 1532.

In Australia, however, the official rate and value for £2000 sterling is 25% more in Australian pounds, namely, £2500. Hence the figures now are as follows: 300 francs or lire equal £25. 1000 francs or lire equal about £83. 6.8. 30,000 francs or lire equal £2500. In many dioceses, however, diocesan statutes allow pastors to expend up to £100 without the written authorization from the ordinary.

With this unit value in mind one can view paragraphs 2 and 3 of canon 1532 in a much clearer light.

> 2. But if the value of the objects involved does not exceed a thousand lire or francs, it is the local ordinary [who gives permission], after he has heard the council of administration, unless the object is of very small value, and with the consent of the interested parties.
>
> 3. Finally, if the value of the objects involved is between 1,000 and 30,000 francs it is the local ordinary [who gives permission], provided he has obtained the consent of the cathedral chapter (diocesan consultors), of the council of administration, and of the interested parties.[61]

It is to be noted that the granting of permission by the bishop without the consent of the diocesan consultors and the council of administration renders the alienation invalid. The bishop cannot supply for their lack of consent.[62]

The same must also be said for the consent of the interested parties. Furthermore, the local ordinary cannot convalidate an alienation that eventuated as invalid because of the non-observance of the formalities required by law.[63] The sum of the 30,000 lire or francs mentioned in paragraph 3 of canon 1532 is now replaced with the 2,000,000 francs or 3,000,000 lire of the October 18, 1952 decree of the Sacred Consistorial Congregation.

> 4. If the object to be alienated is divisible, the petition for permission or consent must specify

[61] Canon 1532, §§ 2, 3.

[62] Cf. S.C.C., 14 ian. 1922—*AAS*, XIV (1922), 160; Bouscaren, *op. cit.*, 1, 730 f.

[63] Cf. S.C.C., 18 maii 1919—*AAS*, XI (1919), 382 f.; Bouscaren, *op. cit.*, 1, 727.

> the portions of it already alienated; otherwise the permission is invalid.[64]

From what has been said about the canons governing the administration and the alienation of church property in general the precaution required by this prescription is evident. The competent superior must be made acquainted with the complete background of the case before he passes judgment on the necessity or the utility of any transaction, and hence *a fortiori* when a church has already been deprived of a portion of its patrimony. No concealment is admissible, as it would endanger the validity of the permission, and hence of the transaction itself.

Canon 1533 applies the formalities detailed in canons 1530-1532 not only to alienation in the strict sense[65] but also to any contract by which the status of the Church might be impaired.

> The formalities required according to the norm of canons 1530-1532 must be observed not only in alienation in the strict sense, but also in the making of any contract by which the condition of the Church may be endangered or its status worsened.[66]

Any contract placing the Church in long term debt is included under the norm of this canon. A pastor, therefore, when he seeks permission for borrowing a loan must also state the current indebtedness of the parish. Prelates and pastors have indeed a full authority for effecting an improvement in the condition of their churches, but they are minus all authority to contribute towards any deterioration of it.[67] A certain deterioration and jeopardy always results from a mortgaging of the property, and sometimes also from the making of donations[68] and the assumption of onerous contracts.[69]

[64] Canon 1532, § 4.
[65] Cf. *supra*, p. 95.
[66] Canon 1533.
[67] Cf. c. 2, X, *de donationibus*, III, 24.
[68] Cf. canon 1535.
[69] Cf. c. 2, X, *de solutionibus*, III, 23.

The IV Plenary Council requires the permission of the ordinary for the contracting of any debt, in conformity of course with the ruling contained in canon 1532.[70] Furthermore, the contracting of debts with the permission of the ordinary must be done in the name of the trustees.[71]

That the Church as a juridical entity and personality[72] can utilize a twofold judicial action, personal or real, for the protection of its rights is stated in canon 1534.

> 1. The Church can enter suit against the person of one who alienates ecclesiastical property without the observance of the requisite formalities, and against his heirs; if the alienation was invalid, it can bring suit against anyone in possession of the property, but the purchaser retains his rights against the one guilty of the unwarranted alienation.[73]

The procedure is different in the case of an invalid alienation from that in the case of an unlawful act. In the former no real transfer takes place, for in the eyes of the law the object of the contract remains as it was before. The object, however, in an unlawful alienation passes into other hands. The only redress which the law offers is punishment of the responsible person with the penalty which the law sets up as a penal sanction. According to canon 1532, §§ 1, 3, this sanction varies with the varying amount of the wrongfully alienated sum, that is, unlawful alienation in the strict sense is punished with unreserved excommunication, if the value of the property was such that for its alienation the permission of the Apostolic See was needed. In accordance with the October 18, 1952, decree of the Sacred Consistorial Congregation, if the value was over 100,000 lire and less than 3,000,000 lire, the principal penalty is loss of office on the part of the administrator. For an ordinary, or for clerics holding some ecclesicatical office, the penalty is a fine equal to twice the value of the property

[70] Cf. *Concil. Plen. Austral. IV*, decr. 665.

[71] *Ibid.*, decr. 676. Cf. *supra*, p. 87, 888.

[72] Cf. canon 1498.

[73] Canon 1534, § 1.

alienated. Other clerics are to be suspended for a period at the discretion of the ordinary.[74]

The object of the real action is to recover the property against anyone who acquired church property that was alienated illegally, even if in good faith. The civil law, however, would not recognize such an action, even though the law here in point forms one of the exceptions to the provision of canon 1529, according to which the Church, in general, canonizes the civil law in the matter of contracts.[75]

The second paragraph of the canon lists those who can file an action for recovery.

> 2. A suit contesting an invalid alienation of ecclesiastical property may be brought by the one who alienated it, by his superior, by the successor of either in office, or, finally, by any cleric attached to the church which has been injured.[76]

The texts from which this canon is taken threatened with penalties the clergy who neglected to denounce the unlawful alienator or donors.[77] The present law, however, is silent about penalties for those who fail to protest.

Another mode of alienation results from the making of donations.

> Prelates and rectors shall not presume to make donations of the movable property of their churches, except small and moderate ones in accordance with the legitimate custom of the place, unless the donations be justified by a reason based on compensation, piety, or Christian charity; otherwise the donation can be revoked by their successors.[78]

Since donations connote contracts[79] and consequently may be upheld by the civil law, it behooves pastors to be both

[74] Cf. canon 2347, 1°-3°.

[75] Cf. canon 1529.

[76] Canon 1534, § 2.

[77] Cf. c. 6, *de rebus ecclesiae alienandis vel non*, III, 13; c. 2, X, *de donationibus*, III, 24.

[78] Canon 1535.

[79] Cf. *supra*, pp. 89 ff.

reasonable and circumspect in such acts of their administration. As a general rule donations are to be small and moderate in accordance with the local custom. Three reasons, however, may justify largesse. The first is: *reward* or *remuneration,* that is, a reward for services rendered to the Church, especially over a period of many years. In this connection one may well recall the ruling and injunction of canon 1524, and the axiom that one must be just before one is generous. The second is: *piety,* which should be gaged in line with the status of the church and its income along with the purpose for which it is given. The third is: *Christian charity,* which should, as far as possible, be as all-embracing as the love with which the spouse of Christ, the Church, is actuated.

The Church as the recipient of donations is treated in canon 1536.

> 1. Unless the contrary is proved it must be presumed that what is given to rectors of churches, even of the churches of religious, is given to the church.[80]

The IV Plenary Council does not permit pastors and rectors of churches, even of the churches of religious, to consider donations their own unless they can prove that these were made explicitly to themselves.[81] It should be noted, furthermore, that this presumption operates in favor of the parish in the case of parishes served by religious.[82] On the contrary, however, stole fees are reserved to the pastor by canon 463. In addition to the usual or the customary fee, if anything extra is given this likewise belongs to him, unless clearly it was given with a view to the individual (*intuitu personae*) to another who had acted for him.[83]

> 2. A donation made to a church cannot be refused by its rector or superior without the permission of the ordinary.

[80] Canon 1536, § 1.

[81] Cf. *Concil. Plen. Austral. IV,* decr. 666.

[82] Cf. canons 533, § 1, 4°; 630, § 3.

[83] Cf. *Concil. Plen. Austral. IV,* decr. 668.

> 3. If a donation is unlawfully refused, for the loss thereby resulting a suit lies for the omission of acceptance (for a *restitutio in integrum*) and for indemnification.
>
> 4. A donation made to a church and legitimately accepted by it cannot be revoked because of the ungrateful attitude of the prelate or rector.[84]

The word "church" in this context means any ecclesiastical moral person according to the norm of canon 1498. The refusal of a donation does not constitute alienation, for the reason simply that the money or the property has not come into the ownership of the church.[85]

Hence the suit will seek, not the actual gift, but indemnification from the party who with consequent injury to the church refused to accept the gift. If, however, the one who had wrongfully refused to accept the gift can purge his wrong by inducing the prospective donor to renew the gift, then no action, so it seems, needs to be taken against him. Still, if the amount of a gift of money is so large that the loss of interest during the time between would amount to a substantial injury to the church, it seems that the one who has wrongfully refused the gift should answer in damages to that extent. It seems that the persons who are duly authorized to file suit are those who receive mention in canon 1534, § 2.

> Sacred objects are not to be lent for a use that is not in keeping with their nature.[86]

This rule follows from the very nature of sacred objects.[87] Traditionally it is absolute and admits of no exception.[88] In practice, therefore, pastors should never allow the church to be used for concerts, lectures, cinematographic presentations and the like, even though these activities

[84] Canon 1536, §§ 2, 3, 4.

[85] Cf. *supra*, Article 2, p. 97, 98.

[86] Canon 1537.

[87] Cf. canon 1497, § 2.

[88] Reg. 51, R.J., in VI°: "Semel Deo dicatum, non est ad usus humanos ulterius transferendum."

be staged for a pious end, or would serve some useful purpose.[89]

ARTICLE 4. MORTGAGES, DEBTS, AND SALE OF ECCLESIASTICAL PROPERTY

> 1. If for a legitimate reason church property must be pledged or mortgaged, or debts have to be contracted, then the lawful superior, whose consent is needed in accordance with the norm of canon 1532, must demand that a previous hearing be given to all interested parties and he must see to it that the debt be paid as soon as it can be done.
>
> 2. For this reason the annual rate of amortization payments shall be designated in advance by the same ordinary.[90]

A *pledge* or *pawn* (*oppignoratio*) is a real contract[91] by which movable goods are handed over to the creditor as collateral security, which *same* goods are to be returned to the pledgor when the debt is paid. The goods handed over are called a pledge.[92] A *mortgage* (*hypotheca*), on the

[89] Cf. *Concil. Plen. Austral. IV*, decr. 514, 515.

[90] Canon 1538, §§ 1, 2.

[91] Cf. *supra*, p. 89.

[92] A pledge *(pignus)* is, under the Anglo-American law, also a contract of bailment involving a chattel (a movable object) which is given under the contract by the debtor to his creditor to secure the payment of the debt. By a mortgage under the English common law, a debtor, to secure payment of his debt, conveyed to the creditor the ownership of immovable property, with the condition that the conveyance would be void on the payment of the debt on a certain day, but with the further condition that default on that day would result in the creditor's obtaining absolute title to the property conveyed. The severity of the rule affecting the time of repayment was gradually relaxed by the rule requiring foreclosure proceedings and the granting of a period of grace for payment. A further relaxation permitted the creditor to recover only the amount of his loan. Some of the States have departed from the legal view that the creditor has a title to the mortgaged property, and the general tendency is toward the new view which they have adopted, namely, that a mortgage merely gives the creditor a lien on the mortgaged property. Cf. Stenger, *The Mortgaging of Church Property*, pp. 69-71.

other hand, is a consensual contract[93] by which immovable goods are so entrusted to a creditor as security for a debt that, if the debt is not paid, he can demand payment due to him before other creditors from the price of the goods mortgaged.[94]

As a detailed examination of the nature of a mortgage is outside the scope of this work the writer confines himself to and holds the common view that a contract of mortgage is not alienation in the strict sense. While it does not involve an absolute and unconditional surrender or transfer of ownership it does, nevertheless, fall within the scope of canon 1533, which is the basis of the present canon, since it is drawn up in legal form (a contract) and gives as security some specific portion of the stable capital or patrimony of the church. Alienation in the strict sense would take place, of course, if the church failed its obligations under the contract and the formalities of canons 1530-32 would then have to be observed.

The canon mentions pawning or mortgaging. In effect the only difference between these two is that the one is used when movable goods are deposited as security and for a short period of time; the other for immovable property as security over a considerably longer period. In actual practice the only goods suitable for pawning or pledging are precious goods which of their very nature require the permission of the Holy See to be used as security or to be alienated.[95] Thus they are put on a par, as far as seeking permission is concerned, with immovable property over the 30,000 francs.[96]

The debts referred to in the canon are those that burden the stable capital of a parish, and not those which are cur-

[93] Cf. *supra*, p. 89.

[94] Cf. Beste, *Introductio in Codicem*, p. 767.

[95] Cf. canon 1632, § 1, 1°.

[96] In view of the decree which the Sacred Consistorial Congregation issued on Oct. 18, 1952, the sum of the 30,000 francs mentioned in the code is now to be interpreted as a sum totalling 2,000,000 francs or 3,000,000 lire. Cf. *supra*, p. 107.

rently encountered during the course of the ordinary parochial administration.[97] The ordinary should see to it that the debt is discharged through systematic repayments, if the church has fixed revenues or rentals, either from the regular deductions therefrom or, if no fixed endowment or revenues are available, as is the case in the majority of churches, then from the establishment of a "sinking fund" for that specific purpose.

Special norms for the sale and exchange of ecclesiastical goods are stated in canon 1539.

> 1. In the sale or exchange of sacred objects no account shall be taken of the consecration or the blessing in the fixing of the price.
> 2. Administrators may exchange so-called bearer securities (*tituli ad latorem*) for other securities that are safer, or at least equally safe and productive, to the exclusion of all semblance of trading or profit-seeking, after they have obtained the consent of the ordinary, of the diocesan council of administration, and of other interested parties.[98]

Sale is a consensual bilateral contract whereby one of the parties transfers or agreees to transfer the ownership of a thing in consideration of a price which the other party obliges himself to pay.[99] Exchange or barter differs from the contract of sale in that both parties exchange goods. In either case there must be a delivery of goods to complete the contract, though constructive delivery suffices.[100]

Further precautions with regard to the sale or the lease of immovable property to the administrators themselves or to their relatives are contained in canon 1540. This new provision in canon law undoubtedly seeks to forestall scandal and to obviate the possibility of favoritism or nepotism. The canon specifies only immovable property, but the very

[97] Cf. canon 1523, 4°, 5°.

[98] Canon 1539, §§ 1, 2.

[99] Cleary, *Canonical Limitations on the Alienation of Church Property*, The Catholic University of America Canon Law Studies, n. 100 (Washington, D.C.: The Catholic University of America, 1936), p. 88.

[100] Cf. Abbo-Hannan, *The Sacred Canons*, II, 744.

restriction implies that due prudence should be used in similar disposals of movable goods.

> Without the special permission of the local ordinary the immovable property of the Church shall not be sold or leased to its administrators or to those who are related to them in the first or second degree of consanguintity or affinity.[101]

Article 5. The Rental, Leasing and Lending of Ecclesiastical Property

Canon 1541 in treating of the leasing of church property reiterates the norms established in former canons for alienation.

> 1. Contracts of lease of any ecclesiastical real estate or land shall not be made except in accordance with the norms of canon 1531, § 2; in such leases there shall always be effective provision for the protection of the established boundaries, for the adequate maintenance of the property, for the due payment of the annual rents, and for appropri ate safeguards regarding the fulfillment of the conditions.[102]

Before leasing ecclesiastical property the administrator should, in keeping with canon 1529, familiarzie himself with the state law regarding such contracts. In matters involving property of considerable value, the legal aspects should obviously be attended to by the diocesan legal advisers in accordance with the general law[103] and provincial decrees.[104] Ordinarily, as is stated in canon 1531, § 2, the land is to be leased through the advertisement of terms as established by appraisal and, with due regard to circumstances, to the highest bidder.

A lease or a contract of rental is a consensual contract whereby a certain price is paid for the use or enjoyment of a determined piece of property for a specified time. In so far as an owner thus temporarily disposes of his right

[101] Canon 1540.

[102] Canon 1541, § 1.

[103] Cf. canons 1520, 1521.

[104] Cf. *Concil. Plen. Austral. IV*, decr. 654.

to use his property the contract is called *rental* (*locatio*); on the part of the lessee, however, it is known as *hire* (*conductio*). Latin authors, when writing of such contracts, specify these two aspects under one head, as they do for the contract of sale and purchase, namely, *contractus locationis-conductionis, contractus emptionis-venditionis.* The use of the word *locatio* is in Anglo-American law reserved for reference simply to movable property or services.[105]

2. In the leasing of ecclesiastical property the norm of canon 1479 shall be observed; moreover, if the value of the lease is in excess of 30,000 lire or francs and the lease runs for more than nine years, Apostolic approval is required; if the lease runs for not more than nine years, the provision enacted in canon 1532, § 3, must be observed.[106]

2°. If the value lies between 1,000 lire and 30,000 lire or francs and the lease runs for more than nine years, the same provision as enacted in canon 1532, § 3, must be observed; if the lease runs for not more than nine years, the norm of canon 1532, § 2, must be observed.[107]

3°. If the value does not exceed 1,000 lire or francs but the lease runs for longer than nine years, the same provision of canon 1532, § 2, shall be observed; if the term of the lease does not exceed a span of nine years, then the lease may be granted by the lawful administrators, who thereupon will notify the ordinary.[108]

The value of 1,000 francs or lire as estimated from the 1952 instruction of the Sacred Consistorial Congregation is £83. 6.8.[109] The prescription of canon 1479 relates to the making of advance payments by the lessee, namely, in the case of the leased property of a benefice. Payments in ad-

[105] Cf. Abbo-Hanan, *The Sacred Canons*, II, 744.

[106] The permission of the local ordinary and the consent of the diocesan consultors, of the diocesan council of administration, and of the interested parties are required.

[107] The permission of the local ordinary, upon consultation with the diocesan council of administration, along with the consent of the interested parties, is required.

[108] Canon 1541, § 2, 1°, 2°, 3°.

[109] Cf. *supra*, p. 102 ff.

vance for more than six months are forbidden without the permission of the local ordinary, who is, in extraordinary cases, to impose adequate guarantees to prevent such a lease from resulting in loss to the pious place or to the successors of the incumbent in the benefice.[110]

The contract of *emphyteusis* or long term lease is treated in canon 1542.

> 1. In a contract of *emphyteusis* involving ecclesiastical property the lessee cannot pay off the rental obligation without the permission of the competent ecclesiastical superior as designated in canon 1532; but if he does pay it off, he shall give the church at least that pecuniary endowment which corresponds to the rental value.
>
> 2. There shall be demanded from the lessee (*emphyteuta*) an adequate guarantee for the payment of the rent and the fulfillment of the conditions imposed; in the very document setting forth the agreement the eccelsiastical forum shall be designated as the arbiter for the settling of controversies that may arise between the parties, and it shall be expressly declared therein that improvements follow the soil (i.e., acrue to the owner of the land).[111]

Emphyteusis is more akin to the idea in English Law of a *long term lease,* e.g., at least beyond a twenty-year period, more particularly conveying the idea of the ninety-nine-year lease that has now, for the most part, fallen into desuetude. Contracts such as those conveyed by the idea of *emphyteusis* in this canon are hardly likely to occur in English-speaking countries where English law is in operation.[112]

The lending of ecclesiastical goods or the granting of loans for consumption, as contemplated in canon 1543, are those which an ecclesiastical moral person makes to another party, not loans which it receives from others.

[110] Canon 1479.

[111] Canon 1542, § 1, § 2.

[112] Cf. Augustine, *A Commentary on the New Code of Canon Law,* VI, 607; Abbo-Hannan, *op. cit.,* II, 746.

> If a fungible thing is so given to another that it becomes his with the obligation that he later return another thing of the same kind, no profit can be taken in virtue of the contract itself; but in the act of giving the fungible thing it is not inherently unlawful to make an agreement for the receipt of a legal profit, unless it is evident that this is exorbitant, or even for the receipt of a greater profit, if a just and proportionate title warrants it.[113]

Fungible goods are those that can be replaced or repaid in kind, as, e.g., a bale of hay for a similar bale lent previously. The morality of charging interest is dealt with at length in moral theology.[114] The Code here makes it clear that it is legal to charge interest on loans according to the usual and legal rate, not indeed by reason of the contract but rather by reason of the risk incurred.

[113] Canon 1543.

[114] Cf. Noldin-Schmitt, *Summa Theologiae Moralis* II, nos. 585 ff.

CHAPTER VI

PIOUS FOUNDATIONS

ARTICLE 1. THE NATURE OF PIOUS FOUNDATIONS AND THEIR ESTABLISHMENT

The IV Plenary Council of Australia, other than reiterating the universal law of the Church as it is stated in canons 1541-1550, has but one decree on pious foundations. Since this concerns their administration, it will be treated in the following article. The general provision contained in decree no. 680 is that those canons in the Code which regulate founded Masses are to be faithfully observed.

A *pious will* has already been defined in the law[1] as any disposal of goods to pious causes, whether it is made in the lifetime of a person or in contemplation of his death. With the term *pious foundations*, on the other hand, there is signified that property, which is given in any way to any moral person in the Church with the obligation, which is perpetual or at least attaches for a prolonged period, of devoting the annual income to the celebration of a certain number of Masses, to the performance of other specified ecclesiastical functions, or to the carrying out of certain works of piety or charity.[2]

The length of time postulated for the creation of a pious foundation is nowhere defined in the law. Some regard forty or fifty years as necessary, others, however, as short a period of time as ten years.[3]

The foundation, lawfully accepted, takes on the nature of a reciprocally binding contract: *do ut facias*.[4]

A reciprocally binding contract is an innominate bilateral

[1] Cf. canon 1513, § 1.

[2] Canon 1544, § 1.

[3] Cf. Beste, *Introductio in Codicem*, p. 769; De Meester, *Compendium*, III, no. 1499.

[4] Canon 1544, § 2.

contract, i.e., one in which each party binds himself to the other to perform something. While there are contracts similar to these in English law the term *contractus synallagmaticus* as used here is not known.[5] It should be noted that in every contract, whether expressed or implied, there must be a mutual or a reciprocal consideration, that is, something must be given or done in exchange for something else. Now, in this innominate bilateral contract, what is given for establishing a pious foundation is a certain sum of money, or at least some temporal goods; what is reciprocated is the performance of certain *spiritual works*. Hence the Code in the following canon establishes the right of the ordinary to act within certain norms to fix the minimum of the endowment and the manner in which the fruits or the returns are to be distributed.

> It is the duty of the local ordinary to prescribe the norms concerning the quantity of the endowment below which a pious foundation cannot be accepted as well as the manner in which the income accruing from it is to be distributed.[6]

In canon 1546 there are enacted additional requisites and precautions whereby ordinaries are to safeguard both the pious foundation that is to be established and the moral person accepting it. These are the written consent of the ordinary and the capability on the part of the institution for fulfilling the work accepted by it.

> 1. In order that foundations of this kind can be accepted by a moral person, there is required the local ordinary's written consent, which he shall not give until he has lawfully ascertained that the moral person is capable of fulfilling both the new obligation which it is about to assume and the previous obligations already assumed; he shall particularly take care that the income shall be entirely adequate for the fulfillment of the attached burdens according to the practice of the individual diocese.
>
> 2. The patron of a church has no right in the

[5] Cf. *supra*, p. 90.

[6] Canon 1545.

> acceptance, in the establishment and in the administration of a foundation.[7]

The acceptance of the foundation by the moral person seems absolutely necessary because of the fact that it is an innominate bilateral contract.[8] The ordinary's consent also seems necessary for validity, since the acceptance is an act of extraordinary administration[9] on the part of the administrator.

Article 2. The Administration of Pious Foundation

The investment and administration of pious foundations are acts of extraordinary administration. Hence, besides the provisions of canon 1527, which in general bind administrators not to act outside their powers (*ultra vires*), the safekeeping and the safe investment of pious foundations are in addition called for in canon 1547.

> Money and movable property, if they be made part of the endowment, shall be immediately deposited in a safe place designated by the ordinary, for the purpose of adequately preserving the money or the value of the movable property, and of safely and profitably investing it as soon as possible in the name of the foundation, with the express and individual mention of the burden assumed, and in accordance with the prudent judgment of the ordinary, given after he has heard the interested parties and the diocesan council of administration.[10]

It is obvious from the wording of the canon that much is left to the prudent judgment of the ordinary. Hence, in the matter of dealing with movable goods, the circumstances and condition of the market will dictate the most secure and profitable course of action. It is to be noted that such goods or the proceeds thereof are to used for the advancement of the pious foundation itself, even though manifestly a greater need is present for other parochial works. In accordance with the ruling of canon 1539, § 2,

[7] Canon 1546, §1, § 2.

[8] Cf. canon 1544, § 2.

[9] Cf. canon 1527, § 1.

[10] Canon 1547.

administrators may exchange the securities for others that are safe or at least equally productive.[11]

> 1. Foundations made orally are to be set down in writing.
> 2. One copy of the articles shall be safely kept in the archives of the curia; another, in the archives of the moral person to which the foundation belongs.[12]

Furthermore, the records of the obligations and of their fulfillment are to be diligently kept by administrators.

> 1. The ruling of canons 1514-1517 and 1525 are to be observed, and there shall be drawn up in every church a schedule of the burdens resulting from the pious foundations, which schedule the rector shall preserve in a safe place.
> 2. Similarly, in addition to the book required by canon 843, § 1 (wherein are recorded the manual offerings for the celebration of Mass), the rector shall keep under his supervision another book, in which shall be recorded all perpetual and temporary obligations, their fulfillment, and also the corresponding offerings, so that an accurate accounting regarding all these matters may be given to the local ordinary.[13]

The IV Plenary Council of Australia especially decreed that in the parochial inventory mention is to made of all pious foundations.

> In the inventory particular mention is to be made of the amount of the capital sum established for founded Masses. In the report concerning the expenses and recipts that must be sent annually to the curia, the manner of the investment itself, the amount of the interest received, and the number of Masses celebrated are to be diligently noted. If any surplus remains, it is to go to the church in which the foundation is made.[14]

The provisions which bind local ordinaries are extended also to religious ordinaries by canon 1550.

[11] Cf. canon 1532, § 2.

[12] Canon 1548.

[13] Canon 1549, § 1, § 2.

[14] *Concil. Plen. Austral. IV*, decr. no. 681.

> In the case of pious foundations in churches belonging to exempt religious, even though they are parochial churches, the rights and duties of the local ordinary as mentioned in canons 1545-1549 belong exclusively to the major superior.[15]

The reduction of obligations arising from pious foundations is reserved to the Apostolic See. Such a reduction may not infrequently become necessary because of the changed circumstances and economic condition of a country or even of an investment.

> 1. The reduction of burdens attached to pious foundations is reserved exclusively to the Apostolic See, unless a contrary provision is contained in the articles of foundation, allowance of course being made for the applicable norm enacted in canon 1517, § 2.
> 2. An indult permitting the reduction of founded Masses does not extend to other Masses due under a contract or to other burdens of a pious foundation.
> 3. A general indult permitting the reduction of the burdens of pious foundations is so to be understood, unless the contrary interpretation is warranted, that the person using the indult shall preferably reduce other burdens rather than Mass obligations.[16]

Canon 1517 authorizes the ordinary, after hearing the interested parties, to make a reduction when the terms no longer can substantially be fulfilled on condition that the administrator has been blameless, with the exception of the obligations that call for the celebration of Masses. In Australia, almost universally, the obligations of Masses are fulfilled by means of the celebration of Low Masses. Special stipends for High Masses are almost unknown, and hence are not considered in the fulfillment of the obligations of Masses. It seems to be a wise precaution, however, in establishing pious foundations that interested parties concede to the ordinary the authority, if and whenever necessary, to commute or even to reduce the number of the obli-

[15] Canon 1550. Cf. also canons 533; 630-31; 1425; 1489.

[16] Canon 1551, § 1, § 2, § 3.

gations. Even in such a case, in accordance with the norm for the modification of last wills, there is required, for the very validity of the act, a justifying necessity for any reduction in the number of Masses normally to be celebrated according to the terms expressed in the charter or articles of the pious foundation.[17]

[17] Cf. *supra*, p. 72, 73.

CONCLUSIONS

1. The right of the Catholic Church to acquire and administer property by all just means allowed to others was officially and practically recognized in Australia consequent upon the passing of the English Acts of Emancipation in 1829.

2. The tenure of property acquired by ecclesiastical corporations is the same as that of other juridical entities. *The corporation aggregate* is favored by state law preference to the *corporation sole* or *fee simple* method of tenure.

3. With the exception of tithes and first fruits the methods of acquiring income and property in the Church follow the general law and practice.

4. The individual is free and unhampered in each and every devise, bequest or legacy made according to the civil law in favor of the Church or any juridical entity in the Church, as is the latter in its acceptance.

5. Conciliar enactments reiterate the universal law for the acquisition and administration of ecclesiastical goods and enlarge its scope by means of added specific prescriptions, patricularly with regard to parochial administration.

6. The local ordinary is obliged to establish a diocesan council of administration. In matters of greater moment its consent is required for the validity of his administrative acts.

7. Pious foundations in Australia, though few in number, follow the general provisions of the Code.

FORM OF WILL

This is the last Will and Testament of me, Thomas Smith, of number thirty-five George Street, Liverpool, Plumber. I give, devise and bequeath all my real and personal property of every description to my wife Mary Smith absolutely. And I appoint the same Mary Smith sole executrix of this my Will, and revoke all Wills by me at any time heretofore made, and declare this writing to be my last Will and Testament. In witness whereof I hereunto set my hand this fourteenth day of March in the year of Our Lord one thousand nine hundred and fifty-seven.

Signed by the said Thomas Smith in the presence of us, who at his request, and in his presence and in the presence of each other, at the same time, have subscribed our names as witnesses.	Charles Davis, 25 North Street, Fairfield, Clerk. George Hunter, 18 Third Avenue, Granville, Grocer.

(The Will must be signed by testator and two (2) witnesses in sight and presence of each other—all three at the same time.)

IF A TESTATOR DESIRES TO ASSIST A DIOCESE OR A CHARITABLE INSTITUTION OR TRUST THE FOLLOWING FORM MAY BE USED:—

I bequeath the sum of .... pounds (£..................) (and/or I bequeath the residue of my real and personal estate) to the Roman Catholic Archbishop (or Bishop) of (name the place and State) for the time being or if there should be no Roman Catholic Archbishop (or Bishop) at the date of my death to the person for the time being administering the Roman Catholic Archdiocese (or Diocese) of (name the place) aforesaid for such charitable purposes within the said Archdiocese (or Diocese) as he shall from time to time determine.

OR

I bequeath the sum of .... pounds (£...................) to the Superior for the time being of (name institution) for the benefit of such institution and I declare that the receipt of the Treasurer for the time being of such institution shall be a sufficient discharge to my executor for such sum.

BIBLIOGRAPHY

SOURCES

Acta Apostolicae Sedis, Commentarium Officiale, Romae, 1909—

Acta Ecclesiae Mediolaniensis, Mediolani, 1599.

Acta et Decreta Concilii Plenarii Baltimorensis Tertii, A.D. MDCCCLXXXIV, Baltimorae: John Murphy, 1886.

Acta et Decreta Concilii Plenarii Americae Latinae, Romae, 1900.

Acta et Decreta Concilii Primi Provinciae Australiensis, A.D. MDCCCXLIV, Sydney; F. Cunninghame &Co., 1847

Acta et Decreta Concilii Secundi Provinciae Australienais, A.D. 1869, Sydney; F. Cunninghame & Co., 1870.

Acta et Decreta Concilii Plenarii Australasiae, Habiti apud Sydney, A.D. 1885, a Sancta Sede Recognita, Sydney; F. Cunninghame & Co., 1887.

Acta et Decreta Concilii Plenarii Australiensis II., Habiti apud Sydney, A.D. 1885, a Sancta Sede Recognita, Sydney; F. Cunninghame & Co., 1898.

Acta et Decreta Concilii Plenarii Australiensis III., Habiti apud Sydney, A.D. 1905, a Sancta Sede Recognita, Sydney; William Brooks & Co., 1907.

Acta Sanctae Sedis, 41 vols., Romae, 1865-1908.

Australasian Catholic Directory, 1956, Sydney; Pellegrini & Co. Pty. Ltd., 1956.

Canon Law Digest, The ed., by T. Lincoln Bouscaren, 3 vols. and Supplements through 1953, 1954 and 1955, Milwaukee: Bruce & Co., 1934-1949-1953-1954-1955-1956.

Codex Iuris Canonici, Pii X Pontificis Maximi iussu digestus, Benedicti Papae XV auctoritate promulgatus, Praefatione, Fontium Annotatione et Indice Analytico-Alphabetico, ab Emo Petri Card. Gasparri Auctus, Romae, 1917. Reimpressio, Westminster, Maryland; The Newman Press, 1954.

Codicis Iuris Canonici Fontes, cura Emi Petri Card. Gasparri editi, 9 vols., Romae (postea Civitate Vaticana): Typis Polyglottis Vaticanis, 1923-1939 (Vols. VII-IX, ed. cura et studio Emi Iustiniani Card. Serédi).

Collectanea Sacrae Congregationis de Propaganda Fide, 2 vols. (Vol. 1, Ann. 1622-1866; Vol. 11, Ann. 1867-1906, Nn. 1300-2317), Romae: Typographia Polyglotta, 1907.

Concilium Plenarium IV Australiae et Novae Zelandiae Habitum apud Sydney, A.D. 1937, Editio Officialis, Manly: The Manly Daily, Pty. Ltd., 1939.

Concilii Plenarii Baltimorensis II., in Ecclesia Metropolitana Baltimorensi, a die VII. ad diem XXI. Octobris, A.D. MDCCCLXVI.,

Habiti, et a Sede Apostolica Recognita, Acta et Decreta, Baltimorae: John Murphy, 1868.

Corpus Iuris Civilis, 3 vols., Vol. 1, *Institutiones,* quas recognovit P. Krueger; *Digesta,* quae recognovit T. Mommsen et retractavit P. Krueger, ed. stereotypa 15., Berolini: Apud Weidmannos, 1928.

Decretales D. Gregorii Papae IX, una cum glossis, Romae, 1582.

Enchiridion Symbolorum Definitionum et Declarationum de Rebus Fidei et Morum, H. Denzinger, C. Bannwart, J. Umberg, editio vigesima sexta, emendata et aucta, Friburgi Brisgoviae: Herder and Co., 1947.

Halsbury's Laws of England, Hailsham's Second Edition, Vol. XI, London; Butterworth & Co. Ltd., 1933.

Leonis XIII, Pontificis Maximi, Acta, 23 vols., Romae: Typographica Vaticana, 1881-1905.

Liber Sextus Decretalium D. Bonifacii Papae VIII, suae integritati cum Clementinis et Extravagantibus, earumque Glossis restitutis; Romae, 1582.

Mansi, Joannes, *Sacrorum Conciliorum Nova et Amplissima Collectio,* 53 vols., Parisiis, 1901-1927.

The Australian Digest, 1825-1947, Being a Digest of the Reported Decisions of the Australian Courts and of Australian Appeals to the Privy Council, 28 vols., Sydney: Australian Law Book Club, 1948.

The Holy Bible, The Old Testament and The New Testament, Published with the Approbation of His Eminence Cardinal Gibbons, Baltimore, Maryland: John Murphy Company, 1914.

The Statutes of Great Britain and Ireland, 10 George IV, 1829, London: His Majesty's Printers, 1829.

The Statutes of Great Britain and Ireland, 2 & 3 William IV, 1832, London: His Majesty's Printers, 1832.

Thesaurus Resolutionum Sacrae Congregationis Concilii, 167 vols., Urbini, 1718-1741; Romae 1741-1908.

Reference Works

Abbo, John A.-Hannan, Jerome D., *The Sacred Canons,* 2 vols., St. Louis; B. Herder Book Co., 1952.

Aquinas, Thomas, St., Doctor Angelicus, *Summa Theologiae,* cura et studio Sac. Petri Caramello, cum textu ex recensione Leonina, Taurini, Romae: Marietti, 1950.

Augustine, Charles, *A Commentary on the New Code of Canon Law,* 2. ed., 8 vols., St. Louis and London, B. Herder Book Co., 1918-1924.

Augustine, Charles, *The Pastor According to the New Code of Canon Law,* St. Louis; B. Hearder Book Co., 1923.

Beste, Udalricus, *Introductio in Codicem*, 3. ed., Collegeville, Minnesota: St. John's Abbey Press, 1946.

Blat, Albertus, *Commentarium Textus Codicis Iuris Canonici*, 5 vols. in 6, Romae: Ex Typographia Pontificia in Instituto Pii IX, 1919-1927.

Bouscaren, T. L.-Ellis, A. C. ,*Canon Law, Text and Commentary*, 2. ed., Milwaukee: Bruce and Co., 1951.

Cavagnis, F., *Institutiones Iuris Publici Ecclesiastici*, 4. ed., 3 vols., Romae, 1906.

Cleary, Joseph F. *Canonical Limitations on the Alienation of Church Property*, The Catholic University of America Canon Law Studies, No. 100, Washington D. C.: The Catholic University of America, 1936.

Comyns, Joseph J., *Papal and Episcopal Administration of Church Property*, The Catholic University of America Canon Law Studies, No. 147, Washington D.C.: The Catholic University of America Press, 1942

Coronata, Mattheus Conte a, *Institutiones Iuris Canonici*, 5 vols., Taurini: Marietti, 1928-1936; Vol. 11, *De Rebus*, 1931.

D'Annibale, J. *Summula theologiae moralis*, 3. ed., 3 vols., Romae: Ex Typographia Polyglotta, 1888-1892.

De Meester, A. *Iuris Canonici et iuris canonico-civilis compendium*, 3 vols. in 4, Brugis: Desclée, 1921-28.

Doheny, William J., *Church Property: Modes of Acquisition*, The Catholic University of America Studies in Canon and Roman Law, No. 41, Washington D.C.: The Catholic University of America, 1927.

Encyclopaedia Britannica, XIII. ed., New York and London: The Encyclopaedia Britannica Inc., New York, 1926.

Ferraris, Lucius, *Prompta Bibliotheca, Canonica, Juridica, Moralis, Theologica, necnon Ascetica, Polemica, Rubricistica, Historica*, ed. Migne, 8 vols., Parisiis, 1860-1863.

Funk, F. X., *Doctrina Duodecim Apostolorum*, Tubingae, 1887.

Goodwine, John A., *The Right of the Church to Acquire Temporal Goods*, The Catholic University of America Canon Law Studies, No. 131, Washington D.C.: The Catholic University of America Press, 1941.

Hannan, J., *The Canon Law of Wills*, Philadelphia: The Dolphin Press, 1934.

Heston, Edward Louis, *The Alienation of Church Property in the United States*, The Catholic University of America Canon Law Studies, No. 132, Washington D. C.: The Catholic University of America Press, 1942.

Kerr, Donald, *The Principles of the Australian Lands Titles (Torrens) System*, Sydney: The Law Book Company of Australasia Limited, 1927.

Laureutius, J., *Institutiones Iuris Ecclesiastici*, Friburgi Brisgoviae, 1908.

Leage, R., *Roman Private Law*, 2. ed., C. H. Ziegler, London: Macmillan, 1930.

McManus, James, *The Administration of Temporal Goods in Religious Institutes*, The Catholic University of America Canon Law Studies, No. 109, Washington D.C.: The Catholic University of America, 1937.

Maitland, Frederick William, *Roman Canon Law in the Church in England, Six Essays*, London: Methuen & Co., 1898.

Migne, P. J., *Patrologiae cursus completus, series Graeca*, 162 vols., Paris, 1857-66.

Migne, P. J., *Patrologiae cursus completus, series Latina*, 221 vols., Paris, 1844-55.

Moran, Patrick Francis Cardinal, *History of the Catholic Church in Australasia*, 2 vols., Sydney: The Oceanic Publishing Company Limited, 1895.

Noldin, H.-Schmitt, A., *Summa Theologiae Moralis iuxta Codicem Iuris Canonici*, 24. ed., 3 vols., Ratisbonae: F. Pustet, 1936.

O'Brien, Ernis M., *The Dawn of Catholicism in Australia*, 2 vols., Sydney: Angus & Robertson Ltd., 1928.

Paton, G. W., *The British Commonwealth. The Development of its Laws and Constitutions*, 2 vols., London: Stevens & Sons, Ltd., 1952.

Pollock, F.-Maitland, F. W., *History of English Law before the Time of Edward I.*, 2 vols., Cambridge: 1895.

Peaslee, Amos J., *Constitutions of Nations*, 2 vols., Sydney: Australian Law Book Club, 1948.

Prümmer, D., *Manuale Iuris Canonici*, 3. ed., Friburgi Brisgoviae: Herder 1922.

Prümmer, D., *Manuale Theologiae Moralis secundum principia S. Thomae Aquinatis*, 3 vols., 10. ed., Barcelona: Herder, 1945.

Quick, John-Garran, Robert Randolph, *The Annotated Constitution of the Australian Commonwealth*, Sydney: Angus & Robertson, 1901.

Rivet, L. *Institutiones Iuris Ecclesiastici*, 2 vols., Romae: 1914.

Sabetti, A.-Barrett, T., *Compendium Theologiae Moralis*, 29. ed., New York: Frederick Pustet Co., Inc., 1920.

Schmalzgrueber, F. *Ius Ecclesiasticum Universum*, 5 vols. in 12, Rome, 1843-1845.

Sherman, C. P., *Roman Law*, 2. ed., 3 vols., New Haven: 1922.

Stenger, J., *The Mortgaging of Church Property*, The Catholic Uinversity of America Canon Law Studies, No. 169, Washington, D.C.: The Catholic University of America Press, 1942.

The Commonwealth Bureau of Census and Statistics, *Year Book of the Commonwealth of Australia, No. 41, 1955*, Canberra, A.C.T., Australia, Government Printer, 1955.

Vermeersch, A.-Creusen, J., *Eptitome Iuris Canonici*, 3 vols., Vol. II, 7. ed., Mechliniae-Romae: H. Dessain, 1954.

Wernz, Franciscus, *Ius Decretalium*, 6 vols., Romae et Prati: 1898-1914.

Wernz, F.-Vidal, P., *Ius Canonicum*, 7 vols. in 8, Romae: Apud Aedes Universitatis Gregorianae, 1923-1938.

Woywood, S.-Smith, E.,*A Practical Commentary on the Code of Canon Law*, rev. ed., 2 vols., New York: J. F. Wagner, Inc., 1948.

Yorston, Robert Keith, *The Australian Commercial Dictionary*, 2. ed., Sydney: The Law Book Co. of Australasia Pty. Ltd., 1950.

Yorston, Robert Keith-Fortesque, Edward E., *Australian Mercantile Law*, 8. ed., Sydney: The Law Book Co. of Australasia Pty. Ltd., 1955.

Periodicals

Periodica de Re Canonica et Morali utilia praesertim Religiosis et Missionariis, Brugis, 1905—

The Ecclesiastical Review (originally *The American Ecclesiastical Review*), Philadelphia, 1889—

Articles

Collins, Lt.-Col. D., "Account of the Colony of New South Wales from January, 1788, to August, 1801," in Moran, *History of the Catholic Church in Australia*, I, 19 ff.

Therry, Mr. Justice R., "Remininescences of New South Wales," London, 1863, in Moran, *History of the Catholic Church in Australia*, I, 15 ff.

Abbreviations

AAS—Acta Apostolicae Sedis.

ASS—Acta Sanctae Sedis.

C.J.—*Corpus Juris.*

C.L.R.—*Crown Law Reports.*

Coll. S.C.P.F.—Collectanea Sacrae Congregationis de Propaganda Fide.

D.—*Digesta* (Iustiniana).

Fontes—Codicis Iuris Canonici Fontes cura . . . Gasparri editi.

L.R.—*Law Reports.*

MGP—Migne, *Patrologia, Series Graeca.*

MPL—Migne, *Patrologia, Series Latina.*

Periodica—Periodica de Re Canonica et Morali, etc.

R.J.—*Regula Juris.*

ALPHABETICAL INDEX

BIOGRAPHICAL NOTE

James Edward Munday was born on February 11, 1917, in Liverpool, New South Wales, Australia. He received his primary education at St. Mary's Convent, Liverpool, and his secondary and high school education at the Christian Brothers' Colleges at Burwood and Lewisham, Sydney, from 1928 until 1933. On March 1, 1934, he entered St. Columba's College, Springwood, where he began the course in Scholastic Philosophy in preparation for the priesthood. In March, 1938, he commenced the study of the Sacred Sciences at St. Patrick's College, Manly, where he was ordained to the priesthood in the Cerretti Memorial Chapel by His Eminence Norman Thomas Cardinal Gilroy, Archbishop of Sydney, on November 29, 1941. After serving in various parishes in the archdiocese, he enrolled in the School of Canon Law at the Catholic University of America in September, 1954. He received the degree of Baccalaureate in Canon Law in June, 1955, and the Licentiate in June, 1956.

CANON LAW STUDIES*

375. Kelleher, Rev. Francis T., A.B., J.C.L., Judicial expenses.
376. Bantigue, Rev. Pedro N., J.C.L., The Provincial Council of Manila of 1771. (Its text followed by a commentary on *Actio* II, *De Episcopis*)
377. Burns, Rev. Dennis J., J.C.L., Matrimonial indissolubility: contrary conditions.
378. Deutsch, Rev. Bernard F., J.C.L., Jurisdiction of pastors in the external forum.
379. Dunnivan, Rev. John P., A.B., J.C.L., Prejudicial attempts in pending litigation.
380. Ernst, Rev. Albert C., A.B., J.C.L., Free admission to church for sacred rites.
381. Frattin, Mr. Peter Louis, J.C.L., The matrimonial impediment of impotence: occlusion of the spermatic ducts and vaginismus.
382. Henry, Rev. Charles W., O.S.B., A.B., S.T.L., J.C.L., Canonical relations between bishops and abbots at the beginning of the tenth century.
383. Hoffman, Rev. Lawrence J., A.B., J.C.L., Clergy conferences: Canon 131.
384. Markham, Rev. James, A.B., S.T.L., J.C.L., The Sacred Congregation of Seminaries and Universities of Studies.
385. McGrath, Rev. John J., A.B., LL.B., J.C.L., A comparative study of crime and its imputability in ecclesiastical criminal law and in American criminal law.
386. McGuire, Rev. James D., O.R.S.A., J.C.L., The postulancy.
387. Munday, Rev. James E., J.C.L., Ecclesiastical Property in Australia and New Zealand.
388. Murphy, Rev. Joseph P., A.B., J.C.L., The laws of the State of New York affecting church property.
389. Pickard, Rev. William M., J.C.L., Judicial experts: a source of evidence in ecclesiastical trials.
390. Ruddy, Rev. James, J.C.L., The Apostolic Constitution *Christus Dominus*: text, translation and commentary, with short annotations on the Motu Proprio *Sacram Communionem.*
391. Vanyo, Rev. Leo. V., A.B., J.C.L., Requisites of intention in the reception of the sacraments.

* For a complete list of the available numbers of this series apply to the Catholic University of America Press, 620 Michigan Avenue, N.E., Washington (17), D.C., for a general catalogue.

www.ingramcontent.com/pod-product-compliance
Lightning Source LLC
LaVergne TN
LVHW050217080826
844660LV00012B/428
* 9 7 8 0 8 1 3 2 2 5 4 7 0 *